WALKING THE SARSEN WAY

STONEHENGE, AVEBURY, SALISBURY AND THE CRANBORNE DROVES WAY

by Steve Davison

JUNIPER HOUSE, MURLEY MOSS,
OXENHOLME ROAD, KENDAL, CUMBRIA LA9 7RL
www.cicerone.co.uk

© Steve Davison 2024
First edition 2024
ISBN: 978 1 78631 126 9

Printed in India by Replika Press Pvt Ltd using responsibly sourced paper.
A catalogue record for this book is available from the British Library.

© Crown copyright and database rights 2024 OS AC0000810376
All photographs are by the author unless otherwise stated.

Updates to this guide

While every effort is made by our authors to ensure the accuracy of guidebooks as they go to print, changes can occur during the lifetime of an edition. Any updates that we know of for this guide will be on the Cicerone website (www.cicerone.co.uk/1126/updates), so please check before planning your trip. We also advise that you check information about such things as transport, accommodation and shops locally. Even rights of way can be altered over time. We are always grateful for information about any discrepancies between a guidebook and the facts on the ground, sent by email to updates@cicerone.co.uk or by post to Cicerone, Juniper House, Murley Moss, Oxenholme Road, Kendal LA9 7RL.

Register your book: To sign up to receive free updates, special offers and GPX files where available, create a Cicerone account and register your purchase via the 'My Account' tab at www.cicerone.co.uk.

Acknowledgement

I would like to thank Tim Lewis, Trustee of The Friends of The Ridgeway and Area Footpath Secretary of the Wiltshire Ramblers, for his help in checking the accuracy of this guide and for his efforts in signing the two routes.

Front cover: The magical outline of Stonehenge (Sarsen Way, Stage 5, Stonehenge loop)

CONTENTS

Map key 4
Route summary table 5

INTRODUCTION 7
The Sarsen Way, Cranborne Droves Way and the Great Chalk Way 8
Geology and nature 9
History 10
When to walk and equipment 12
Getting to and staying along the route 13
Maps and GPS 14
Safety 14
Waymarking and access 15
Using this guide 16
Planning your walk 17

THE SARSEN WAY 19
Stage 1   Coate Water to Barbury Castle 20
Stage 2   Barbury Castle to Overton Hill 27
Stage 3   Overton Hill to Upavon 38
Stage 4   Upavon to Netheravon 51
Stage 5   Netheravon to Amesbury 57
Stage 6   Amesbury to Salisbury Cathedral 69

THE CRANBORNE DROVES WAY 81
Stage 1   Salisbury Cathedral to Cow Down Hill 82
Stage 2   Cow Down Hill to Win Green or Shaftesbury 93

Appendix A   Useful contacts 102
Appendix B   Selected accommodation near the route 103
Appendix C   Further reading 107
Appendix D   Stage facilities planner 108

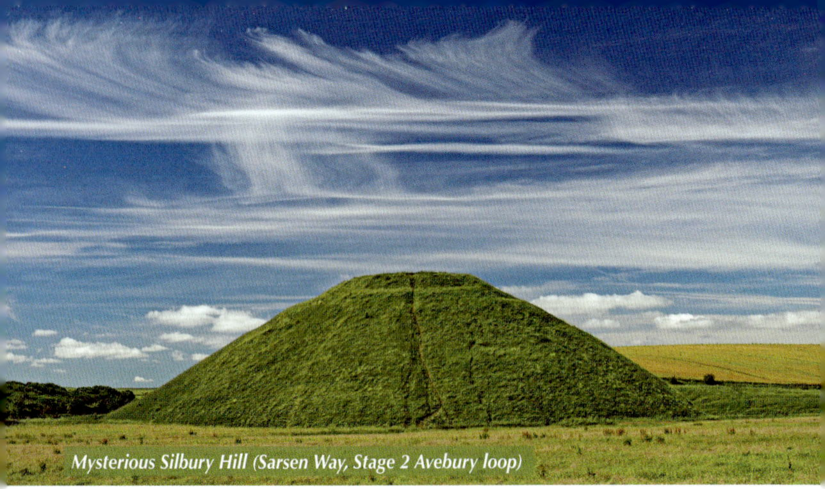

Mysterious Silbury Hill (Sarsen Way, Stage 2 Avebury loop)

Route symbols on OS map extracts
(for OS legend see printed OS maps)

 route
alternative route
link route/detour
 start/finish point
 start point
 finish point
 alternative start/finish point
 alternative start point
 alternative finish point
 route direction

Features on the overview map

county/unitary boundary
urban area
 National Landscape
eg *North Wessex Downs*

SCALE: 1:50,000

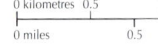

GPX files for all routes can be downloaded free at www.cicerone.co.uk/1126/GPX.

○ hotel/B&B/guesthouse ▲ campsite   refreshments ⊕ grocery shop
◉ outdoor shop ■ train station   bus service   ATM

ROUTE SUMMARY TABLE

The Sarsen Way

Stage	Start	Finish	Distance	Ascent	Time	Page
1	Coate Water (SU 177 827)	Barbury Castle (SU 157 760)	11.3km (7 miles)	220m	3¼hr	20
2	Barbury Castle (SU 157 760)	Overton Hill (SU 118 680)	10.5km (6½ miles)	90m	2¾hr	27
3	Overton Hill (SU 118 680)	Upavon (SU 134 550)	19.3km (12 miles)	230m	5¼hr	38
4	Upavon (SU 134 550)	Netheravon (SU 147 490)	10.9km (7 miles)	190m	3¼hr	51
5	Netheravon (SU 147 490)	Amesbury (SU 152 414)	10.6km (6½ miles)	125m	3hr	57
6	Amesbury (SU 152 414)	Salisbury Cathedral (SU 142 296)	16.3km (10 miles)	255m	4½hr	69
Totals			79km (49 miles)	1110m	22hr	

Variant sections – additional distances, ascent and times to standard stages

Stage	Variant	Distance	Ascent	Time	Page
2	Avebury loop	4.8km (3 miles)	60m	1¼hr	32
3	Wansdyke and Alton Barnes White Horse loop	2.4km (1½ miles)	45m	¾hr	41
5	Stonehenge loop	9km (5½ miles)	145m	2½hr	61

Cranborne Droves Way

Stage	Start	Finish	Distance	Ascent	Time	Page
1	Salisbury Cathedral (SU 142 296)	Cow Down Hill (SU 023 216)	17.3km (10¾ miles)	325m	5hr	82
2	Cow Down Hill (SU 023 216)	Win Green (ST 924 206) or Shaftesbury (ST 862 229)	10.7km (6¾ miles) or 19.2km (12 miles)	205m or 380m	3hr or 5½hr	93
Totals			28km (17½ miles) or 36.5km (22¾ miles)	530m or 705m	8hr or 10½hr	

Some of the sarsen stones that make up the stone circle at Avebury (Sarsen Way, Stage 2 Avebury loop)

INTRODUCTION

The Alton Barnes White Horse (Sarsen Way, Stage 3)

Five thousand years ago, the rolling chalk landscape of Wiltshire between Swindon and Salisbury was, for more than a millennium, a scene of frenzied building work. Tracing a route through these now-peaceful downs and linking the greatest of England's prehistoric sites – Avebury and Stonehenge – the Sarsen Way takes you on a journey through this prehistoric landscape, passing Neolithic henges and stone circles, Bronze Age barrows and Iron Age hill forts. But that's not all, there are also ancient churches and the majestic medieval cathedral at Salisbury to visit along the way, as well as far-reaching views, tranquil riverside scenes, picturesque villages and cosy pubs to enjoy.

The Cranborne Droves Way sets out from Salisbury heading across the Harnham Water Meadows before meandering over the rolling downland of the Cranborne Chase National Landscape to reach a highpoint at Win Green from where there are some great views. An optional ending at the Dorset market town of Shaftesbury, home to the ruins of a once great abbey founded by Alfred the Great, is also provided.

This guidebook provides all the information needed to follow the Sarsen Way and the Cranborne Droves Way in either direction. Whether you

WALKING THE SARSEN WAY

do one continuous walk, or prefer to spread the pleasure over several visits, you are sure to enjoy your journey along these fascinating and historic routes through Wiltshire.

THE SARSEN WAY, CRANBORNE DROVES WAY AND THE GREAT CHALK WAY

The Sarsen Way

The Sarsen Way long-distance route runs from Coate Water Country Park on the outskirts of Swindon to Salisbury – a total of 79km. However, the route described in this guide has several optional detours that visit Avebury, the Wansdyke and Alton Barnes White Horse, and Stonehenge making a maximum length of 95.2km. The route passes over comparatively gentle terrain, each stage having less than 260m of ascent.

The Sarsen Way has been developed by The Friends of The Ridgeway, a registered charity that has campaigned for over 40 years to preserve the unique character of the ancient 'ridgeway' tracks that form the Great Chalk Way across Southern England, including The Ridgeway National Trail. The route of the Sarsen Way follows parts of three existing long-distance routes; the Ridgeway from Barbury Castle to Overton Hill; the White Horse Trail across the Vale of Pewsey; and the Pewsey Avon Trail from Manningford Abbots to Salisbury.

The Cranborne Droves Way

The Cranborne Droves Way is a 28km route linking the end of the Sarsen Way at Salisbury to the Wessex

The Old Mill at Harnham (Cranborne Droves Way, Stage 1)

Ridgeway at Win Green. An optional ending at Shaftesbury, that is not part of the Cranborne Droves Way, is also described; this option adds 8.5km. The Cranborne Droves Way consists of an amalgamation of three ancient routes: the Old Shaftesbury Drove; the Ox Drove; and Akling Dyke, a former Roman road. Like the Sarsen Way, the Cranborne Droves Way passes over comparatively gentle terrain, each stage having less than 330m of ascent.

The Great Chalk Way

The Great Chalk Way follows a ridge of chalk from Lyme Regis on Dorset's Jurassic Coast to the Wash in Norfolk that is believed to be England's oldest coast-to-coast route. From prehistoric times through to the medieval period, this would have been the safest way of travelling, avoiding the impenetrable forests in the valleys below; today this route, which is around 645km long, is a combination of footpaths, bridleways, byways and the occasional road. Along its length it is packed with historic sights and great views.

The Great Chalk Way (www.greatchalkway.org.uk) consists of several distinct long-distance paths, each retaining its own identity and waymarks. The routes are:

- **Peddars Way National Trail** – following the route of a Roman road for 79km from Holme-next-the-Sea on the North Norfolk coast to Knettishall Heath Country Park on the Norfolk/Suffolk border. Route marking: National Trail acorn (www.nationaltrail.co.uk/en_GB/trails/peddars-way-and-norfolk-coast-path).
- **Icknield Way** – running for 177km from Knettishall Heath Country Park to Ivinghoe Beacon in the Chiltern Hills National Landscape. Route marking: waymarks with an image of a Neolithic stone axe (www.icknieldwaypath.co.uk).
- **Ridgeway National Trail** – a 139km national trail running between Ivinghoe Beacon in the Chiltern Hills National Landscape and Overton Hill near Avebury in the North Wessex Downs National Landscape. Route marking: National Trail acorn (www.nationaltrail.co.uk/en_GB/trails/the-ridgeway).
- **Sarsen Way and Cranborne Droves Way** – covered in this guide.
- **Wessex Ridgeway** – covering 220km from Marlborough in Wiltshire via Win Green to the Dorset coast at Lyme Regis. Route marking: waymarks with an image of a Wyvern, a two-legged dragon associated with the ancient kingdom of Wessex (www.dorsetcouncil.gov.uk/sport-leisure/walking/walking-in-west-dorset/wessex-ridgeway).

GEOLOGY AND NATURE

The geology of the area is derived from the seas that once covered southern England and the sediments that were laid down at that time. The predominant feature – one that forms the rolling contours of the downs – is a thick layer of Upper Cretaceous chalk (99–65 million years ago), composed of incredible numbers of tiny fossil skeletons of algae, called coccoliths.

Associated with the chalk are irregular silica concretions known as flints. Our prehistoric ancestors used flint to make a range of tools, and it has also been widely used as a building material. A natural process of irregular hardening within the sandy beds that overlay the chalk produced blocks of tough sandstone that are more resistant to erosion. These are the famous sarsens that were used in the construction of the Neolithic stone circles at Avebury and Stonehenge; a great number of sarsens can be seen lying in the fields at Fyfield Down National Nature Reserve.

The Sarsen Way meanders through a patchwork of open chalk grassland, broad-leaved woodland and farmland, and there are plenty of opportunities for catching glimpses of local wildlife including foxes, deer and the more elusive badger. During the summer, the grasslands are home to a myriad of butterflies and plants, as well as traditional farmland birds; high above, the silhouette of a buzzard or red kite might be seen. Along the rivers and waterways walkers will probably be accompanied by ducks and mute swans – or may be lucky enough to catch sight of the elusive otter or a flash of blue as a kingfisher speeds by.

HISTORY

The earliest inhabitants of the area were nomadic hunter-gatherers who travelled through the wooded landscape over 10,000 years ago. However, by the Neolithic period (4200–2200BC) a farming lifestyle was developing, permanent camps were being constructed and areas of land cleared for crops and animals. This was the period when the great monuments at Avebury and Stonehenge came into being. The Bronze Age (2200–750BC) saw further developments of these iconic sites as well as the building of numerous characteristic round barrows. During the Iron Age (750BC–AD43) defensive hill forts such as Barbury Castle and Old Sarum were built.

The Romans left little visible evidence in the region, although they did construct a number of roads, including one past Silbury Hill (now the A4). They also built a town at Old Sarum where a number of Roman roads met, including the Portway that ran north-east to Calleva and Ackling Dyke which headed south-west to Badbury Rings (Vindocladia); parts of this former road are followed by the Cranborne Droves Way.

In the early part of the Anglo-Saxon period, following the demise of the Roman Empire in Britain around AD410, the Wansdyke

St Leonard's Church, Bulford (Sarsen Way, Stage 5)

– a massive linear earthwork, part of which stretches across the Marlborough Downs above the Vale of Pewsey – was constructed. In the 9th century Alfred the Great founded a great abbey at Shaftesbury; sadly this was destroyed by Henry VIII in the 16th century. A large part of the Cranborne Droves Way follows an ancient high-level trackway across the downs, known as the Ox Drove. No one knows its real age, maybe it was medieval, or Anglo-Saxon, or maybe it could be much older, but it has been used for moving livestock for centuries.

The Norman period (from 1066) was characterised by motte and bailey castles, such as the one at Old Sarum, as well as monasteries and churches with Romanesque rounded arches over windows and doorways; many churches in the area have their roots in the Norman period, having replaced earlier Saxon structures.

Prosperity and growth in the late 12th and 13th centuries led to the expansion of towns including Salisbury and the building of its impressive medieval cathedral. Much more recently, transport improved with the opening of the Kennet and Avon Canal, quickly followed by the arrival of the railways. During the first and second world wars a number of airfields were built, including one at Netheravon, while Salisbury Plain was commandeered as a military training area, which still continues to this day. A short selection of books that give varying amounts of

The impressive earthworks of Barbury Castle, a former Iron Age hill fort (Sarsen Way, Stage 2)

detail about some of the historical sites that can be seen along the Sarsen Way and Cranborne Droves Way is detailed in Appendix C.

WHEN TO WALK AND EQUIPMENT

The walk can be undertaken at any time of the year, although walking between early spring and the end of autumn offers the chance of more settled weather and better walking conditions. Periods of wet weather can make parts of the route (especially the Cranborne Droves Way) muddy in places.

Always choose clothing suitable for the season, such as a waterproof jacket, comfortable and waterproof footwear and a comfortable rucksack. On wet days, gaiters or waterproof trousers can also be very useful; during the summer nettles can cause a problem on some narrow paths. It's also worth carrying a basic first aid kit to deal with minor incidents.

Places where refreshments and food may be available (pubs, cafés and shops) are mentioned in the box at the start of each stage description (some of these are located along the route, while others involve short detours (3km or less) off-route). However, there is no guarantee that any particular establishment will be open when required, and walkers should carry enough food and water for the day with them.

Mobile phone signals should be available along the route, though reception can be limited in parts. Internet access via wi-fi may be available from accommodation providers, pubs, cafés and tourist information centres, though these are typically off the route. Post offices, banks and ATMs are typically available at towns along the route, while only some villages offer one or more of these facilities.

GETTING TO AND STAYING ALONG THE ROUTE

The nearest mainline train station to Coate Water is Swindon, on the line from London Paddington to the south-west and south Wales. Local buses operate daily between Swindon town centre and Coate Water Country Park (east-bound stop) or Chiseldon. National Express coaches running between London Victoria and Bath stop at Coate Water (A4259). Salisbury has rail services on the line between London Waterloo and the south-west. National Express services operate to London.

Between Swindon and Salisbury, Salisbury Reds (www.salisburyreds.co.uk) operate route X5. This follows the A346 south to Marlborough, calling at Chiseldon, and then follows the A345 to Salisbury with intermediate stops including Enford, Netheravon, Figheldean, Bulford, Durrington, Amesbury and Old Sarum.

Between Salisbury and Shaftesbury, Salisbury Reds operates route 29. This calls at Bishopstone, Broad Chalke, Bowerchalke, Ebbesbourne Wake, Alvediston, Berwick St John (all located slightly off the Cranborne Droves Way) and Ludwell.

For anyone wishing to drive, there is parking (either a car park or on-street) available near to the start and end of each stage. Always remember to park considerately, and be aware that theft from parked cars does occur, so do not leave anything valuable in your car.

Both routes offer a range of accommodation from campsites to

Ruins of an 11th-century Norman motte and bailey castle within the Iron Age earthworks at Old Sarum (Sarsen Way, Stage 6)

B&Bs, pubs with rooms to hotels; places where accommodation may be available are given in the information box at the start of each stage description. Some of these places are located along the route, while others involve detours. A brief list of some accommodation close to the route is given in Appendix B; up-to-date details are available from Visit Wiltshire and local tourist information centres – see Appendix A.

Protecting the countryside

While you are out enjoying these routes, please respect the countryside and follow the Countryside Code:
- Be safe – plan ahead and follow any signs
- Leave gates and property as you find them
- Protect plants and animals, and take your litter home
- Keep dogs under close control
- Consider other people

The routes described in the guide pass a number of scheduled monuments that may be easily damaged without due care, so:
- Do not disturb, walk over, damage, use metal detectors on, or remove any objects from any scheduled monument sites
- Always follow marked routes

MAPS AND GPS

A good map, preferably at a scale of 1:25,000, should always be carried when out walking; a compass is also useful for both orientating the map and knowing your direction. The Ordnance Survey (www.shop.ordnancesurvey.co.uk) offer two series of maps – the 1:50,000 Landranger® series and the more detailed 1:25,000 Explorer® series. The Ordnance Survey maps covering the Sarsen Way and Cranborne Droves Way are:
- 1:50,000 Landranger maps: 173 (Swindon and Devizes) and 184 (Salisbury and The Plain); map 183 (Yeovil and Frome) is required for the Shaftesbury extension only
- 1:25,000 Explorer maps: 169 (Cirencester and Swindon), 157 (Marlborough and Savernake Forest), 130 (Salisbury and Stonehenge) and 118 (Shaftesbury and Cranborne Chase)

Maps are also available to download to a handheld GPS device or smartphone with GPS (there are a number of apps available). These devices can prove very useful; however, batteries can run out of power, so always carry a map. Even if you don't have maps on your phone, there is a free app – OS Locate – that is worth downloading, as this can give you a grid reference that you can use to find your location on a paper map.

SAFETY

The route passes through fairly gentle terrain; however, it is worth remembering that the chalky clay can become slippery when wet and

WAYMARKING AND ACCESS

that stages can be easily shortened if required. Always take extra care when crossing or walking along roads, using pavements where they are provided, or walking on the right (facing oncoming traffic) if there is no pavement, but take extra care on blind corners.

Some parts of the walk pass through fields where cattle may be present. Follow the latest advice: do not walk between cows and young calves. If you feel threatened, move away calmly; do not panic or make sudden noises; and, if possible, find an alternative route. If you are walking with a dog and livestock become aggressive, let the dog off the lead and take care of your own safety first; your dog will likely make its own way out of the field and back to you safely.

In case of a serious accident, call 999 or the European emergency number – 112, and ask for the police, ambulance or fire service depending on the nature of the accident.

WAYMARKING AND ACCESS

The routes described in this guide follow normal rights of way with standard waymarking and both the Sarsen Way and Cranborne Droves Way have also been waymarked using their official logos. The descriptions in this guide, along with the map extracts and the signage on the ground, mean that route finding should not cause any major problems; however, it is recommended that walkers also carry the relevant Ordnance Survey Explorer map.

Rights of way are indicated on signage as follows:
- **Footpaths** Yellow arrow – walkers only
- **Bridleways** Blue arrow – walkers, cyclists and horse riders

Sarsen Way waymark (left) and Cranborne Droves Way waymark (right)

- **Restricted byways** Purple arrow – walkers, cyclists, horse riders and carriage drivers
- **Byways** Red arrow – same as restricted byways plus motorcycles and motorised vehicles

USING THIS GUIDE

The two long-distance routes are split into stages of varying length. Navigation should be fairly straightforward as both routes use designated rights of way, lanes and roads.

A box at the start of each route gives key information such as the start and finish points, the walk distance (km/miles rounded to the nearest 0.1km or ¼ mile), the amount of ascent and an estimate of the time it will take to complete the walk; this information can also be found in the Route Summary Table at the start of the book. Brief details of places offering refreshments, public transport and accommodation are also provided.

Each stage begins with a short introduction providing a brief summary of the stage, identifying any major points of interest, including towns and villages. The route is then described. Throughout the route text you will find key landmarks highlighted in bold type; there is also additional information provided about the places of interest. A full reverse route description is provided for each stage.

The maps in this guide are extracts from the Ordnance Survey 1:50,000 Landranger series maps. The stages have been marked on to the maps, along with any detours. These maps have a scale of 2cm to 1km.

Times and distances

The distances quoted in the text have been measured from OS Explorer maps; note that the heights quoted on the maps are in metres and the grid lines are spaced at intervals of 1km. Distances in the route information boxes are given in metric first, with approximate imperial conversions rounded to the nearest ¼, ½, ¾ or whole number. Estimated walking times are based on a walking speed of 4km per hour (2½ miles per hour), plus 10 minutes per 100m (300ft) of ascent. These are the figures I use when walking, but – of course – some people walk faster and some slower. The estimated walking times should be treated as the minimum amount of walking time required to undertake the route, and they do not include any time for rests, lunch, photography, consulting the map or guidebook, or simply admiring the view. Poor weather, or walking over wet ground, can also make the walk take longer.

GPX tracks

GPX tracks for the routes in this guidebook are available to download free at www.cicerone.co.uk/1126/GPX. If you have not bought the book through the Cicerone website, or if you have bought the book without opening an account, please register your purchase in your Cicerone library to access GPX and route update information.

A GPS device is an excellent aid to navigation, but you should also carry a map. GPX files are provided in good faith, but in view of the profusion of formats and devices, neither the author nor the publisher accepts responsibility for their use. We provide files in a single standard GPX format that works on most devices and systems, but you may need to convert files to your preferred format using a GPX converter such as www.gpsvisualizer.com or one of the many other apps and online converters available.

PLANNING YOUR WALK

For your own enjoyment and convenience, plan your walk carefully in advance. This guide details both the Sarsen Way and Cranborne Droves Way; the Sarsen Way has been split into six stages ranging from 10.5km to 21.7km depending on the route taken; the Cranborne Droves Way has been split into two stages ranging from 10.7km to 19.2km depending on the route taken – see the Route Summary Tables. These are not intended to be individual day sections, but the start and end points coincide with places that either offer parking, transport or accommodation facilities locally (see the Stage Facilities Planner for facilities near the routes). It is up to you to decide how far you want to go each day – whether that means combining two stages or just undertaking part of a stage.

Sarsen Way
- **Stage 1** – from Coate Water Country Park on the outskirts of Swindon the route climbs up to Barbury Castle, where the remains of an Iron Age hill fort offer commanding views
- **Stage 2** – follows The Ridgeway National Trail south to Overton Hill; an alternative loop visits the remarkable prehistoric sites at Avebury
- **Stage 3** – an undulating stage, heads across the Vale of Pewsey following the Kennet and Avon Canal for a time before meeting up with the River Avon to finish at Upavon
- **Stage 4** – a shorter stage along the River Avon valley visiting Casterley Camp on the edge of Salisbury Plain before passing through picturesque villages to end at Netheravon
- **Stage 5** – the route continues along the River Avon valley to end at Amesbury; an optional (longer) loop visits the impressive sites of Durrington Walls, Woodhenge and Stonehenge
- **Stage 6** – heads to the former Iron Age hill fort at Old Sarum, later used by the Normans as a fortified castle before continuing to Salisbury's impressive medieval cathedral, marking the end of the Sarsen Way

Cranborne Droves Way

- **Stage 1** – from Salisbury Cathedral the route crosses the River Nadder and River Ebble heading through Cranborne Chase to Cow Down Hill near Bowerchalke

- **Stage 2** – the route continues west following tracks and lanes along the ridge top route to arrive at Win Green for a great view marking the end of the Cranborne Droves Way; from here you can continue to Shaftesbury

The Sarsen Way - Example Schedule

Day	Start	Finish	Distance	Hr Min
1	Coate Water	Overton Hill	21.8km (13½ miles) (including Avebury 26.6km (16½ miles))	6hr (7¼hr including Avebury)
2	Overton Hill	Upavon	19.3km (12 miles) (including Alton Barnes White Horse 21.7km (13½ miles))	5¼hr (6hr including Alton Barnes White Horse)
3	Upavon	Amesbury	21.5km (13½ miles) (including Stonehenge 30.5km (19 miles))	6¼hr (8½hr including Stonehenge)
4	Amesbury	Salisbury Cathedral	16.3km (10 miles)	4½hr

The Cranborne Droves Way - Example Schedule

Day	Start	Finish	Distance	Hr Min
1	Salisbury Cathedral	Cow Down Hill	17.3km (10¾ miles)	5hr
2	Cow Down Hill	Shaftesbury	19.2km (12 miles)	5½hr

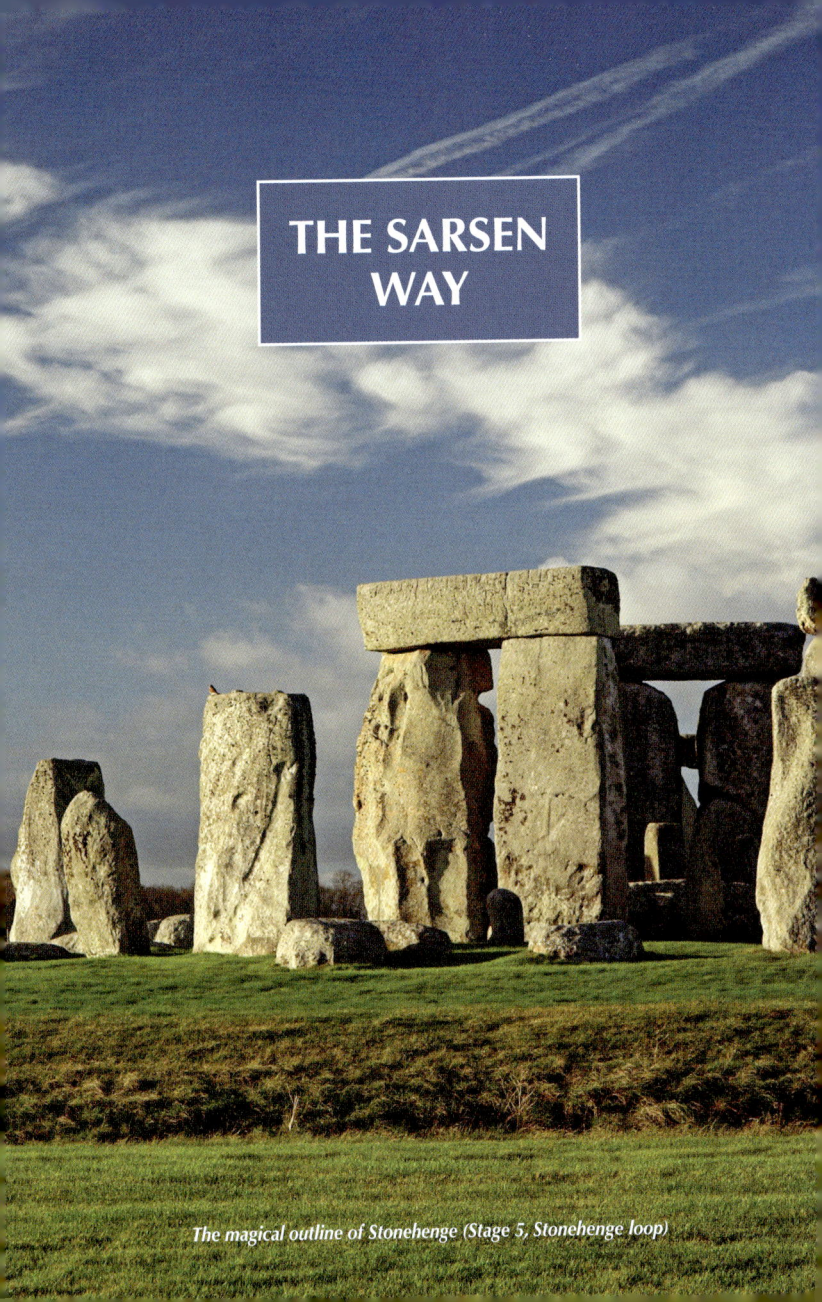

THE SARSEN WAY

The magical outline of Stonehenge (Stage 5, Stonehenge loop)

STAGE 1
Coate Water to Barbury Castle

Start	Coate Water Country Park café (SU 177 827)
Finish	Barbury Castle Country Park car park (SU 157 760)
Distance	11.3km (7 miles)
Ascent	220m
Time	3¼hr
Maps	OS Explorer 169 and 157
Refreshments	Swindon, Coate Water and Chiseldon
Public transport	Swindon has a rail station with local bus links (daily) to Queen's Drive near Coate Water; west-bound buses (including long-distance) stop on Marlborough Road; there are also bus links to Chiseldon from Swindon
Accommodation	Swindon; Chiseldon

From Coate Water Country Park, on the southern outskirts of Swindon, the route heads south following part of the National Cycle Network route 45. After crossing the footbridge over the M4 the walk follows part of an old railway that used to run between Swindon and Marlborough, passing through Chiseldon on the way. The route then heads along a byway up over Burderop Down to Barbury Castle.

Walkers arriving by bus

From Coate Water east-bound stop on Queen's Drive follow the tarred path south through two underpasses and continue to reach the café at Coate Water Country Park. From the west-bound bus stop (Sun Inn) on Marlborough Road, which includes long-distance buses, head west along the pavement and turn left along Day House Lane for 200m, then right (NCN 45 and footpath) to Coate Water. On arriving at the lake, keep left (water on the right); to visit the café turn right.

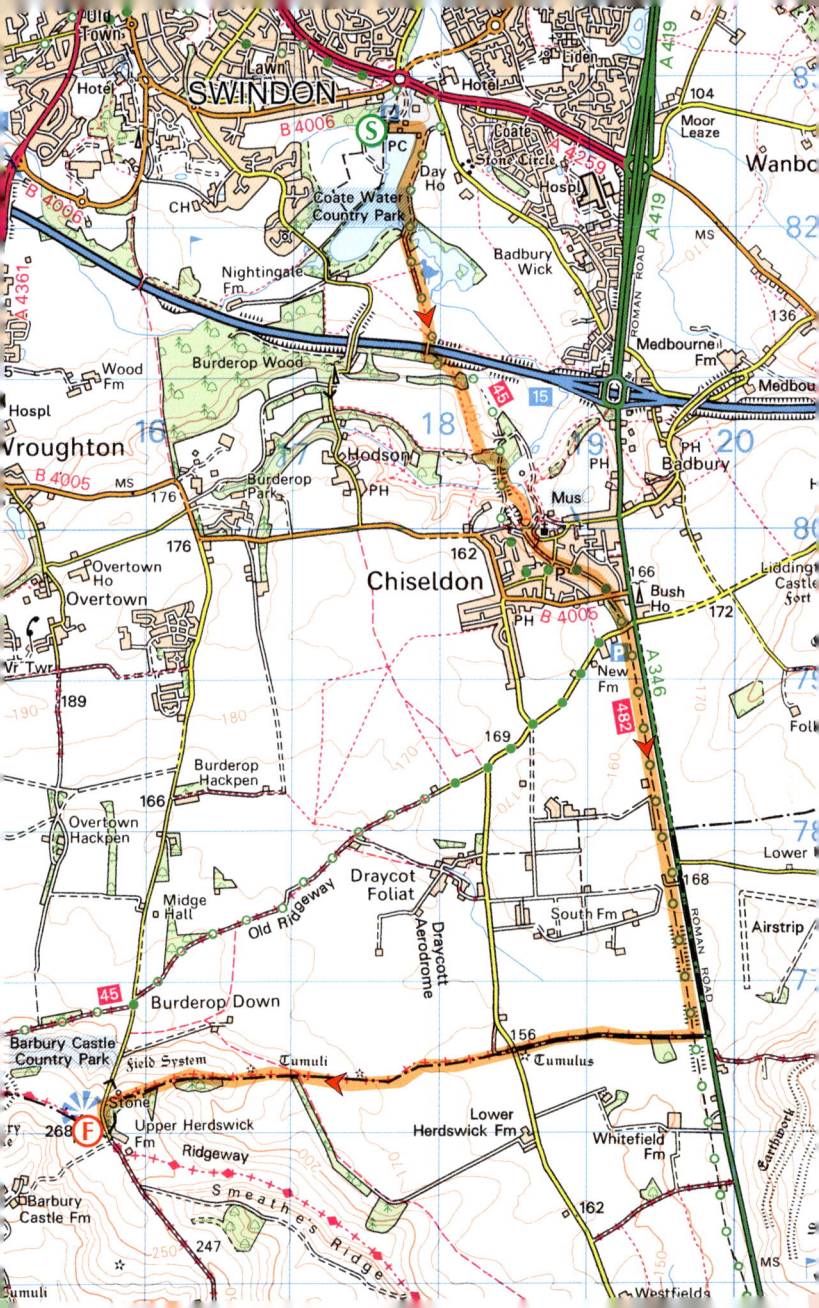

WALKING THE SARSEN WAY

Main route

Stand with the Coate Water café on your right looking south over Coate Water and turn left, keeping the water on your right and follow the path as it soon curves right. ◂ Continue southwards along either the wide cycle path or the waterside footpath, keeping the water on the right.

At the corner a path to the left leads to the Richard Jefferies Museum; while just outside the park on the A4259 there is the Sun Inn (accommodation).

Coate Water, constructed in the 1820s to provide water for the Wiltshire and Berkshire Canal, now forms part of the Coate Water Country Park. The Victorian writer Richard Jefferies (1848–87), noted for his depiction of English rural life, was born at Coate, and the old farmhouse where he grew up is now a museum dedicated to his life and works (www.richardjefferies.org). To the east of Coate Water, on Day House Lane, are the scant remains of a late Neolithic/early Bronze Age stone circle consisting of five recumbent sarsen stones in a field opposite **Day House** (private, no access); records show there were nine stones back in the 19th century.

Coate Water with its former diving platform, on the outskirts of Swindon – start or end point of the Sarsen Way

Stage 1 – Coate Water to Barbury Castle

Cross the cycle/foot bridge and bear left (NCN 45). Later dogleg right and left and continue along the tarred route. Cross the bridge over the M4 motorway and continue along the surfaced foot/cycle path for 75m, then turn right through a kissing gate. ▶ Head diagonally left up across the field, pass through another kissing gate and continue up through woodland to a field. Follow the right-hand edge to the corner, then keep ahead down to a three-way junction and turn left. Cross over the cycle path and take the path opposite, signposted to Chiseldon, heading downhill.

Go through a kissing gate and continue up through the field to another kissing gate in the far-left corner; ignore a path off to the left across the stream on the way. Keep ahead through trees to a junction of paths at the Washpool in **Chiseldon**. Continue ahead; over to the right is a disused railway bridge. Follow the surfaced path up to a junction (steps to left) and dogleg left and right to continue up the surfaced path. Pass a row of cottages (left) and continue up Stroud's Hill (site of the former rail station), passing a parking area and a sarsen stone (both on your right) to a junction; to the right is a shop. Head up Station Road (bus stop for services to Swindon and Marlborough) to a junction with New Street (B4005); 600m to the right is a shop.

Alternatively, continue along the combined foot and cycle path (NCN 45) to a junction on the left signposted to Chiseldon.

> **Chiseldon** is located at the head of a coombe with springs, known as the Washpool; the Saxon name Ceosel Dene means 'stony valley'. The railway arrived in 1881 with the opening of the Swindon, Marlborough and Andover Railway; the line closed in 1961, and part of the disused trackbed now forms the Chiseldon and Marlborough Railway Path. In 2004 the Chiseldon Cauldrons, a unique collection of 12 Iron Age cooking pots or cauldrons (Europe's largest such collection), were discovered nearby. From 1914 until 1960 the parish was home to Chiseldon Camp (now demolished), which originally opened to train soldiers for World War 1.

After leaving the Chiseldon and Marlborough Railway Path the route follows a byway towards Burderop Down

The road to the right later becomes a track (byway) known as the Old Ridgeway (NCN 45) that joins the Ridgeway National Trail just west of Barbury Castle.

Cross the B4005 and take the cycle path opposite to a minor road; ahead on the left is the Three Trees farm shop and café. ◀ Having crossed the minor road, continue southwards along the disused railway track (NCN 482), running parallel to the A346 for 2.8km.

Turn right at a crossing byway and after 1.2km cross a minor road to continue along the byway. At a crossing bridleway turn right, then immediately bear left. At the fingerpost, cross a stile and go through scrub to a second stile. Follow the left-hand field margin up Burderop Down. Cross a third stile and continue alongside the fence (left), passing a large **memorial stone** on the way (right), then cross a stile at the corner. Turn left up the minor road for 125m and then turn right to enter the **Barbury Castle Country Park** car park (toilet facilities).

The **memorial stone** (a large sarsen boulder with plaques) commemorates two local writers – Richard Jefferies (mentioned earlier) and Alfred Williams (1877–1930). Williams was dubbed 'the hammerman poet' as he used to work in the Great Western Railway factory at Swindon.

NORTHBOUND – STAGE 1 – BARBURY CASTLE TO COATE WATER

REVERSE ROUTE – BARBURY CASTLE TO COATE WATER

From Barbury Castle the route heads over Burderop Down before following part of an old railway that used to run between Swindon and Marlborough, passing through Chiseldon on the way. After crossing the footbridge over the M4 the walk continues northwards to end the stage and the journey along the Sarsen Way at Coate Water Country Park, on the southern outskirts of Swindon.

Exit the car park at Barbury Castle Country Park and turn left down the access road for 125m and then turn right over a stile (byway). Continue alongside the right-hand boundary, soon passing the **memorial stone** on Burderop Down (left). Continue downhill, crossing a stile on the way, then go over another stile at the bottom. Go through the scrub and over a third stile. Keep ahead to a bridleway and dogleg right and left to continue down the byway. Cross straight over the minor road and continue along the byway to a junction with a disused railway track (NCN 482). Turn left along this for 2.8km to a minor road at **Chiseldon**; to the right is a farm shop

The memorial stone commemorating two local writers – Richard Jefferies and Alfred Williams – on Burderop Down

and café. Cross straight over and keep ahead, then cross over the B4005 and follow Station Road opposite.

At the four-way road junction (to the left is a shop), keep ahead down Stroud's Hill. After passing a parking area (left), follow the pavement past a row of cottages (right) to a path junction. Keep ahead down the surfaced path through the Washpool to a three-way split and take the middle path; to the left is a disused railway bridge. Follow the path through the trees, go through a kissing gate and continue down through the field, ignoring a path off to the right. Leave through another kissing gate in the far-left corner and head uphill to the railway path (NCN 45). Cross the tarred path and follow a path opposite. Alternatively, turn right and follow the combined foot/cycle path down to the bridge over the M4 motorway. At the three-way junction, turn right uphill and continue along the left-hand field edge. Continue through the trees, then a kissing gate and down across the field to another kissing gate in the bottom left corner. Turn left along the NCN 45 and cross the bridge over the M4 motorway.

Follow the tarred route and after a right and left dogleg continue along the track to a junction at **Coate Water Country Park**. Bear right across the bridge and continue, keeping Coate Water over to the left. Follow the path as it curves left round the end of the lake; a path to the right leads to the Richard Jefferies Museum. Continue alongside the water to the café and the end of the Sarsen Way; the car park is on the right.

For bus connections from Queen's Drive

Continue north along the combined path and shortly before the road fork right to head through the underpass (B4006) to a path junction, either turn left to reach the westbound bus stop (buses to Swindon town centre) or keep ahead through the next underpass and turn left to the eastbound bus stop (buses to Marlborough and Salisbury). For long-distance coaches, on reaching the northern end of Coate Water follow the NCN 45 as it bears right to Day House Lane and turn left to the A4259; the bus stop is opposite, across the road.

STAGE 2
Barbury Castle to Overton Hill

Start	Barbury Castle Country Park car park (SU 157 760)
Finish	Overton Hill car park on A4 (SU 118 680)
Distance	10.5km (6½ miles); via Avebury 15.3km (9½ miles)
Ascent	90m; via Avebury 150m
Time	2¾hr; via Avebury 4hr
Maps	OS Explorer 157
Refreshments	Broad Hinton, Winterbourne Bassett, Winterbourne Monkton, Avebury and Beckhampton (all off-route, except Avebury if following the optional Avebury loop)
Public transport	Buses from Swindon call at Avebury; National Express buses (402) between London and Frome stop at Beckhampton
Accommodation	Winterbourne Monkton (off route); Avebury and Avebury Trusloe (both on or near Avebury loop); East Kennett

This stage follows the Ridgeway National Trail from the lofty heights of Barbury Castle southwards to Overton Hill. On the way you can visit the Hackpen Hill White Horse or take a detour to the fascinating sarsen-strewn landscape of Fyfield Down National Nature Reserve. Walkers may also take an alternative loop through Avebury that passes the world-renowned stone circle and henge and other impressive prehistoric sites.

Head through the Barbury Castle Country Park car park, passing the toilet block, and pass through two gates to reach the earthworks of **Barbury Castle**; the Sarsen Way now follows the Ridgeway National Trail for 9.3km to Overton Hill near Avebury. Keep ahead through the centre of the hill fort to the western edge, although a detour along the ramparts gives some great views.

Looking towards Barbury Castle; the Sarsen Way follows the Ridgeway between Overton Hill and Barbury Castle

The imposing Iron Age earthworks of **Barbury Castle** offer commanding views. In the sixth century, Barbury Castle is thought to have been where the Britons were defeated at the Battle of Beranburgh (Beran Byrig) in AD556. To the north, below the downs, is the former World War 2 Wroughton Airfield; the hangars are now part of the British Science Museum.

A gate on the right gives access to the Hackpen Hill White Horse cut by Henry Eatwell, Parish Clerk of Broad Hinton and a local publican, to commemorate the coronation of Queen Victoria in 1838.

Follow the track down to a lane and turn right along this for 40m, then turn left up the track as it curves to the left. Continue along the fairly level track to a **car park** and minor road, passing three picturesque circular beech copses on the way; shortly before the car park the White Horse Trail joins from the right (this gives access to Broad Hinton and the Crown pub (3.1km each way)). Cross over the minor road and follow the track over **Hackpen Hill**. ◄ Continue along the Ridgeway; later a byway on the right leads down to Winterbourne Bassett and the Winterbourne pub (2.5km each way).

The track makes a dogleg as it passes Berwick Bassett, or Brick Kiln, dewpond, where the **White Horse**

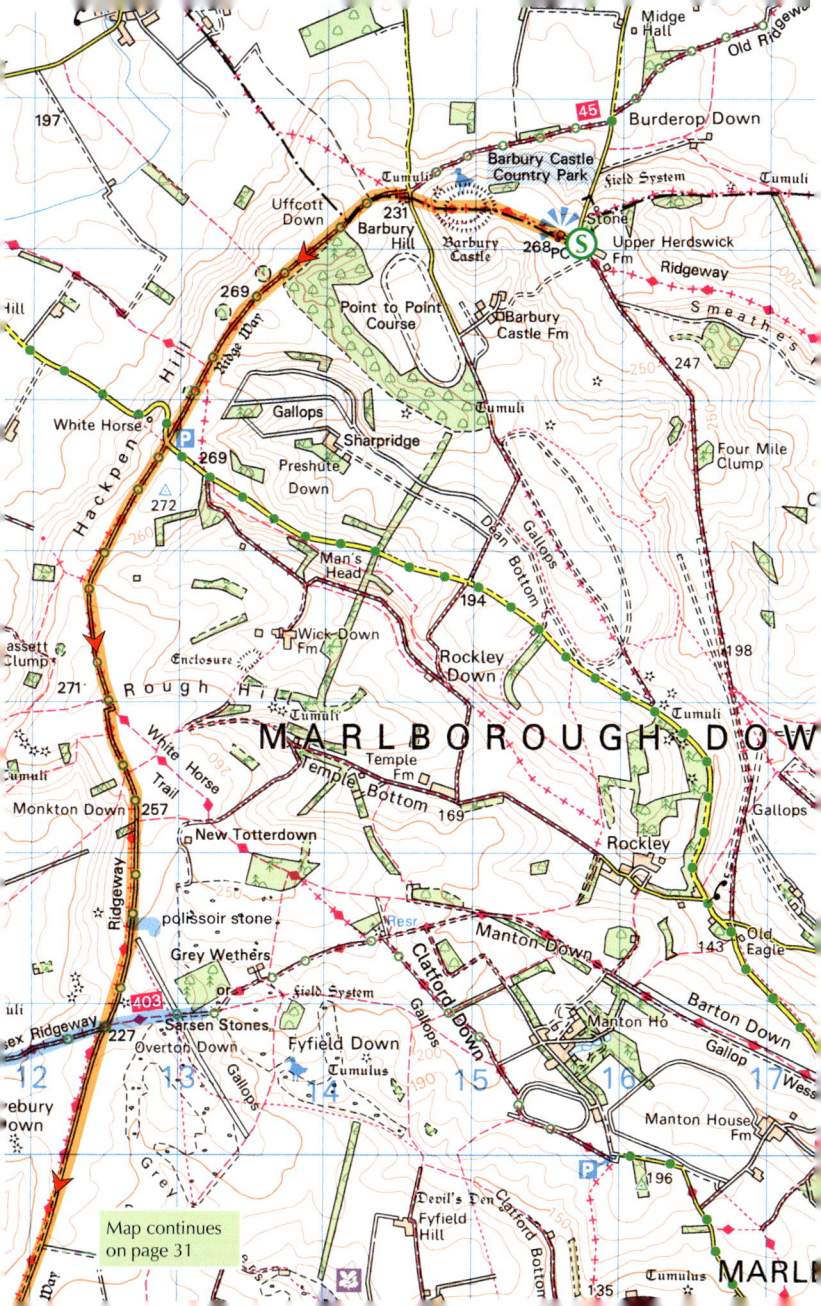

Walking the Sarsen Way

Follow a short detour to visit the polissoir, or polishing, stone

The monument was built in 1845 by the third Marquis of Lansdowne and commemorates Sir William Petty, a well-known 17th-century economist, scientist and philosopher.

Trail forks left; a bridleway off to the right leads down to Winterbourne Monkton and the New Inn (accommodation; 2.9km each way). The Sarsen Way continues to follow the Ridgeway southwards with views to the west including the Lansdowne Monument on Cherhill Down. ◄ About 1.4km south of the dewpond there is a gate on the left from where a short detour leads to the polissoir stone.

Detour to the polissoir stone
Turn left through the gate (SU 126 715), follow the left-hand fence for 150m and then turn right for 50m to a large, flat sarsen stone beside some gorse bushes (SU 1284 7150); retrace your steps through the gate and turn left. The stone, or polissoir, displays several grooves and a smoothed area that were formed by Neolithic people as they sharpened and polished their stone axes several thousand years ago.

Main route continues
Continue southwards to a cross-junction with the Herepath/Green Street (**Wessex Ridgeway**), on Overton Down. ◄ From here you have three choices: a short detour to the left leads to the sarsen-strewn landscape of Fyfield Down National Nature Reserve (NNR) – see below; the track to the right heads down to Avebury (see

This was an Anglo-Saxon army route – 'herepath' literally means 'army path'.

Take a detour to explore the sarsen-strewn landscape of Fyfield Down NNR below Delling Copse

detour); while the Sarsen Way goes straight on for 2.8km to end the stage at the car park on **Overton Hill**. ▶

Detour to Fyfield Down NNR
At the cross-junction, turn left through the gate, passing a sign for Fyfield Down NNR and head eastwards

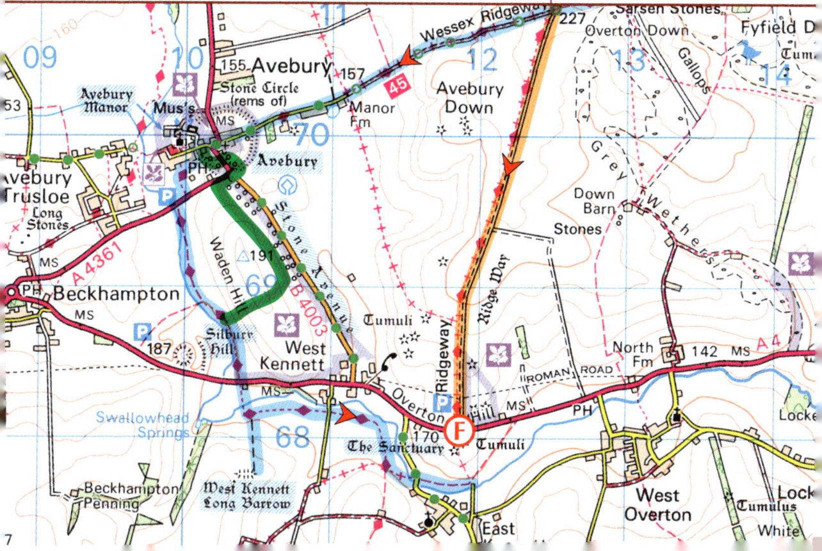

To the left of the car park are several early Bronze Age burial mounds or round barrows.

WALKING THE SARSEN WAY

across the field. Go through gates either side of a gallop to reach a viewpoint just south of Delling Copse (1.5km return); you can explore further if time permits. Here the chalk grassland is littered with the largest collection of **sarsen stones** in Britain. Known locally as 'grey wethers', as from a distance they look like sheep (a 'wether' is a castrated ram or male sheep), these stones are all that remains of a hard silica sandstone layer that was formed over the underlying chalk during the early Tertiary period, 50 million years ago. Subsequent erosion broke the layer into pieces, creating the sarsens. Used in ancient times for building purposes, today they support communities of rare lichen and moss.

The Avebury loop

At the cross-junction turn right down the Herepath/Green Street (**Wessex Ridgeway**), towards **Avebury**, passing

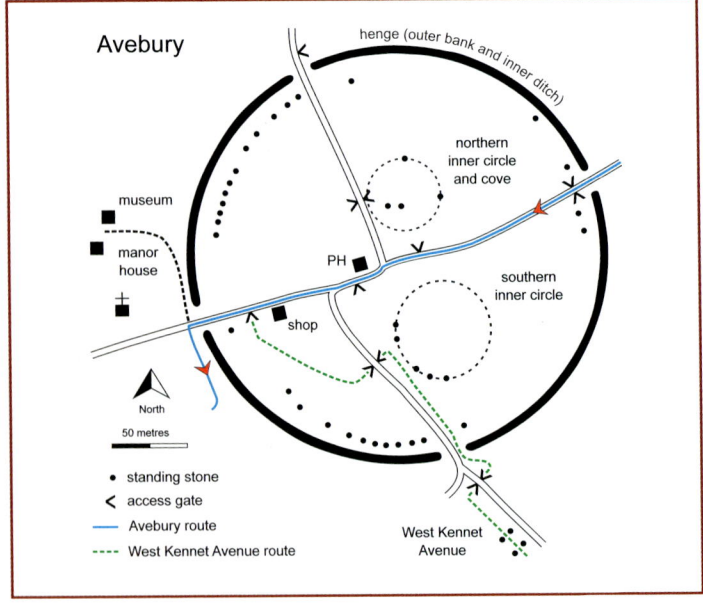

through the henge earthworks to a road junction with the A4361. Cross straight over and pass just left of the Red Lion pub. Continue along the High Street and 50m after the village shop (left) turn left along an enclosed path; a track to the right off the High Street leads to Avebury Manor and the Alexander Keiller Museum, further along the High Street is St James' Church.

AVEBURY

West Kennet Avenue (Avebury loop)

Avebury is well worth exploring and together with Stonehenge is a designated World Heritage Site. The most impressive feature at Avebury is the large henge, a type of Neolithic earthwork, dating from 2600BC, consisting of a circular outer bank and inner ditch (a defensive hill fort has an outer ditch and inner bank). Within this structure is the outer stone circle, one of Europe's largest stone circles, originally marked with 98 sarsen stones, along with two smaller inner stone circles and part of the present village. Linking the henge with the Sanctuary (see Stage 3) is the 2.5km-long West Kennet Avenue, which originally consisted of 100 pairs of standing stones (see detour below). The Alexander Keiller Museum, which houses archaeological finds from the area, is named after Alexander Keiller, heir to the Dundee-based marmalade business, who was responsible for excavating many of the sites at Avebury in the 1930s. Nearby is the 16th-century Avebury Manor, once the home of Alexander Keiller; for more information, visit: www.nationaltrust.org.uk/visit/wiltshire/avebury. St James' Church was altered by the Normans, but retains its tall Anglo-Saxon nave; above the lych gate is the scallop shell symbol of St James, the patron saint of pilgrims and of the Camino de Santiago.

West Kennet Avenue detour

To visit the West Kennet Avenue turn left through a gate after the shop. Follow the path to the left, go through a gate, cross the road (A4361) and through a gate. Turn right and once past the trees, turn right through another gate, cross the minor road and go through a final gate to access the **West Kennet Avenue**. Retrace your steps, or continue alongside the avenue for 800m to the far left-hand corner, go through two gates to enter the adjacent field and turn right over **Waden Hill** (from the top there is a great view of Silbury Hill) before heading downhill to join the main route beside the River Kennet and turn left.

Avebury loop continues
To continue with the main loop, after turning left along the enclosed path follow it as it swings right, then left and continue through the car park. Turn right along the A4361 for 40m, then turn left across the road, go through a gate and follow the bridleway to a junction. Keep ahead along the path, keeping the River Kennet on the right. Over to the right is the unmistakable outline of Silbury Hill (note that there is no access to the hill). ◄

On the way, the detour via the West Kennet Avenue, joins from the left having come over Waden Hill.

The 40m-high **Silbury Hill** is the largest man-made prehistoric mound in Europe, built around 2400BC (late Neolithic), at a similar time to the Avebury stone circle. No one really knows why it was built, although local legend attributes the mound to the devil. He was planning to dump a load of earth on nearby Marlborough, but was stopped by the priests at Avebury, while in another version it's a cobbler who thwarts the devil.

Mysterious Silbury Hill (Avebury loop)

With care, cross the A4 (small parking area) and turn left for 30m, then go right through a gate and follow a track southwards. After crossing the River Kennet bear left for 50m to a large oak tree; from here turn right to visit the **West Kennett Long Barrow**, then retrace your steps to the fence and turn right (400m each way).

West Kennett Long Barrow is one of the largest and most impressive Neolithic chambered tombs in Britain, dating from 3600BC. During excavations the partial remains of at least 46 individuals, along with pottery, beads and stone implements, were found.

Follow the fence along the left edge of the field to a gate, then continue along the track. Cross the lane and stile to follow the hedge on your right as it curves right. Go through a gate, then follow the tree-shaded path to a junction and turn left along a track to a minor road. Go left over the bridge and immediately turn right following a bridleway along the right-hand field margin to a junction with a byway, rejoining the Sarsen Way. Some 400m up to the left is **Overton Hill** car park (across the A4) and the Sanctuary; the onward route (Stage 3) turns right towards East Kennett.

West Kennet Long Barrow – one of the largest Neolithic chambered tombs in Britain (Avebury loop)

REVERSE ROUTE – OVERTON HILL TO BARBURY CASTLE

> This stage follows the Ridgeway National Trail from Overton Hill northwards to the impressive earthworks of Barbury Castle. On the way you can take a detour to the fascinating sarsen-strewn landscape of Fyfield Down National Nature Reserve or visit the Hackpen Hill White Horse. Walkers may also take an alternative loop through Avebury that passes a number of impressive prehistoric sites including the world-renowned henge and stone circle.

Before setting out on the stage, you need to decide whether to follow the alternative Avebury loop or head straight along the Sarsen Way.

To follow the Sarsen Way stand in the car park at Overton Hill with the A4 behind you and head north along the Ridgeway for 2.8km to a cross-junction and gate on the right. The Avebury loop joins from the left (see details below); the detour to the sarsen-strewn Fyfield Down NNR turns right through a gate (1.5km return). Continue northwards along the Ridgeway, later bearing right and left past Berwick Bassett (or Brick Kiln) dewpond; a bridleway to the left leads down to Winterbourne Monkton (pub and accommodation; 2.9km each way) and the **White Horse Trail** joins from the right.

Keep ahead over Berwick Bassett Down; a byway on the left leads down to Winterbourne Bassett (pub; 2.5km each way). Continue over **Hackpen Hill** to a minor road; a gate on the left gives access to the Hackpen Hill White Horse carving. Cross straight over, pass the car park and continue, passing three distinctive circular beech copses; after the first clump the White Horse Trail turns left down to Broad Hinton (pub; 3.1km each way). Continue along the Ridgeway as its curves to the right to a minor road. Turn right for 40m, then turn left through a gate. Continue uphill, passing the earthworks of **Barbury Castle**. Go through a gate and follow the fence on the right before going through another gate to end the stage at the **Barbury Castle Country Park** car park (toilets).

Avebury loop

To follow the Avebury loop head south from **Overton Hill** car park and with care, cross over the A4. Follow the byway opposite, with the Sanctuary on the right, down to a junction, just before the bridge over the River Kennet and turn right along the bridleway, following the field edge to a minor road. If you are heading north towards Overton Hill and wish to follow the Avebury loop you should turn left at the junction and follow the bridleway along the field edge. Turn left and after crossing the River Kennet turn right along a track (byway).

Northbound – Stage 2 – Overton Hill to Barbury Castle

At a cross-junction turn right (path), now following the White Horse Trail. Go through a gate and continue alongside the hedge on the left to a stile. Cross the minor road and follow the track opposite, then cross a stile and continue along the right-hand field edge to a large oak tree; from here turn left to visit the **West Kennett Long Barrow**, then retrace your steps to the fence (400m each way) and turn left.

Follow the fence (which is on your right) for 50m, then turn right. Cross the River Kennet and continue along the track to a gate. Turn left alongside the A4 (small parking area) for 30m and then, with care, turn right across the road. Go through the gate and follow the path (River Kennet on the left); over to the left is Silbury Hill. To continue via the West Kennet Avenue turn right at the field corner (see later description). At a junction keep ahead along the bridleway (River Kennet on left) to the A4361. Turn right and then turn left across the road to enter the car park. Head to the far-right corner and follow the path to a junction. Keep right, following the enclosed path to the main street in **Avebury**; diagonally across the street is the access track for the museum and Avebury Manor, to the left is St James' Church.

Turn right along the main street; the alternative route via the West Kennet Avenue joins from the right. Continue to a junction, keep ahead past the Red Lion pub (left) and cross straight over the A4361 to follow the minor road opposite (Herepath/Green Street; **Wessex Ridgeway**), passing through the earthworks. Follow the lane, passing buildings and keep ahead up the track to a junction with the Ridgeway National Trail; the gate opposite gives access to Fyfield Down NNR. To continue along the Sarsen Way turn left.

Alternative route via West Kennet Avenue

Having turned right at the field corner head over **Waden Hill** and down to the field corner beside the B4003. Turn left through two gates and follow the stone avenue, running parallel with the road. At the far-right corner, turn right through a gate, cross the road and go through a gate. Turn left, following the fence on the left and turn left through a gate. Cross the road, go through a gate and bear half-right to another gate. Now turn right along the main street in **Avebury** towards the Red Lion pub.

STAGE 3
Overton Hill to Upavon

Start	Overton Hill car park (SU 118 680)
Finish	Upavon High Street (SU 134 550)
Distance	19.3km (12 miles); via Alton Barnes White Horse 21.7km (13½ miles)
Ascent	230m; via Alton Barnes White Horse 275m
Time	5¼hr; via Alton Barnes White Horse 6hr
Maps	OS Explorer 157 and 130
Refreshments	Honeystreet, All Cannings (off-route), North Newnton and Upavon
Public transport	Avebury (see Stage 2); North Newnton and Upavon have bus services to Swindon and Salisbury
Accommodation	Avebury and surrounding villages; East Kennett; Honeystreet; All Cannings (off-route); Bottlesford (off-route); Wilcot (off-route); North Newnton and Upavon

The Sarsen Way continues southwards through East Kennett before steadily climbing the chalk downs, passing through the earthworks of the Wansdyke on the way; from Walkers Hill, views extend across the Vale of Pewsey to Salisbury Plain. After dropping down through the neighbouring hamlets of Alton Barnes and Alton Priors the route wanders along the Kennet and Avon Canal for a while before following the River Avon valley to Upavon.

From Overton Hill car park head south, carefully crossing the A4, and take the byway (track) opposite, passing just left of **The Sanctuary** down to a junction. ◄

The alternative loop via Avebury rejoins the Sarsen Way here from the right.

The Sanctuary, which dates from 3000BC, consisted of concentric timber and stone circles. We know from the writings of John Aubrey that in 1648 many of the stones were still standing; however, within 100 years the site was destroyed (the stones, like many others at ancient sites, were used as a

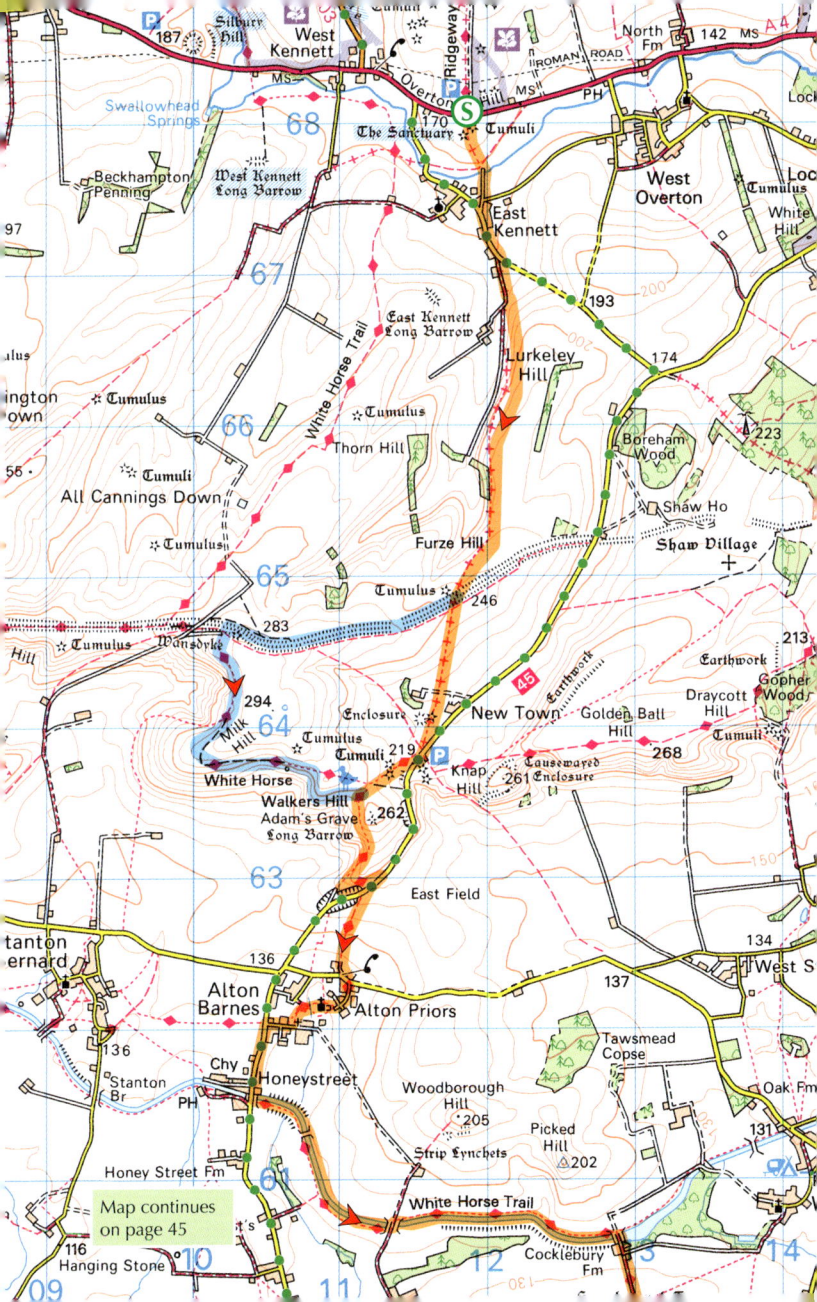

The view looking north from Lurkeley Hill

Note: the route up Lurkeley Hill does not follow the byway as shown on OS maps (as of January 2024) but rather follows a farm track just to the east of the open access land boundary fence.

source of building material). All that remains today are concrete blocks marking where the timbers and stones once stood.

Bear left and right, then cross the River Kennet and continue along the lane, keeping ahead at a junction; left goes to West Overton. At the next junction bear left along the main street through **East Kennett**. At the last house on the right (Hill House), fork right and continue along a track (byway) for 300m, passing some barns (right). At a junction, turn left and follow the track up **Lurkeley Hill** for 2km to a junction with a bridleway at the tree-shaded remains of the Wansdyke. As you climb the views open out to the right (west) and north, including the Lansdowne Monument near Cherhill and further round Silbury Hill. ◄

The **Wansdyke** (or 'Woden's Dyke'), is a series of linear earthworks that date back to at least Saxon times. The impressive eastern Wansdyke runs through Wiltshire from Savernake Forest across the Marlborough Downs above the Vale of Pewsey to Morgan's Hill. The western Wansdyke runs through Somerset from Monkton Combe to Maes Knoll hill fort. Between these sections is the former Roman road that ran between London and Bath.

Stage 3 – Overton Hill to Upavon

Here there is a choice to be made: either take the detour along the Wansdyke (see below) or keep ahead along the Sarsen Way as it descends through three fields (fence on left) to the lower left corner next to a gate, with the road and a car park on your left. ▶ Do not go through the gate on your left to the road, but instead, keep ahead through a kissing gate and follow a permissive path diagonally right through the field. Go through a gate on the right and bear half-left (south-west) uphill, passing through a gate on the way to reach a slight col (SU 111 635) and path junction just to the right of **Adam's Grave** (a Neolithic long barrow or burial mound) on the top of Walkers Hill. ▶

Wansdyke and Alton Barnes White Horse detour

Turn right along the Wansdyke Path for 1.6km to reach a track with a view of the **Wansdyke** earthwork stretching out across the downs. Turn left through a gate to enter Pewsey Downs NNR (information board). Follow the White Horse Trail as it contours round **Milk Hill** (highest point in Wiltshire) before passing above the **Alton Barnes White Horse** to rejoin the Sarsen Way at the col just before Walkers Hill and Adam's Grave. The white horse carving was commissioned by Robert Pile in 1812; the figure underwent a major renovation in 2010.

Across the road, a waymarked route leads up to the earthworks of a Neolithic causewayed camp crowning Knap Hill (600m each way).

The path to the right leads to the Alton Barnes White Horse (500m each way) and is also the return route used by the Wansdyke detour.

Looking out across the Vale of Pewsey to Salisbury Plain from Walkers Hill

WALKING THE SARSEN WAY

Main route continues

After admiring the view across the Vale of Pewsey, follow a good path down from the col (slope down to the right and Walkers Hill/Adam's Grave up to the left) to a gate. ◄ Do not go through the gate, but turn left, staying in the field and follow the hedge on your right, parallel with road (right) for 325m to a gate. Turn sharp right through this and shortly go through another gate, then walk down the road for 75m (care required). Turn left across the road and go through a field entrance.

Follow the tree-shaded bridleway downhill to a lane in **Alton Priors**. Go left for 10m to a junction and turn right. ◄ At the end of the lane go through the turnstile and continue across the field, keeping right of the church to a junction; to visit the church turn left.

> Pop inside **Alton Priors** Norman All Saints' Church, cared for by the Churches Conservation Trust, to see some fine Jacobean carved wooden choir stalls, a tomb-chest of William Button (died 1590), and two sarsen stones hidden under a trapdoor in the floor. These may be from an earlier sacred site – early Christian churches were sometimes built on existing religious sites. Outside in the churchyard stands an ancient yew tree (another pagan symbol) said to be well over 1000 years old.

Keep ahead along the cobbled path, crossing two footbridges with turnstiles and continue to a path junction mid-field. Here, either go straight on and leave through a turnstile then turn right along the lane or, to visit the church, turn left to leave through a gate with the church on the left and then turn right along the lane. ◄

Follow the lane through **Alton Barnes** to a T-junction and turn left along the road towards **Honeystreet**; the fields to the right of the road were the site of the former World War 2 RAF Alton Barnes. Fifty metres before crossing the Kennet and Avon Canal, a track on the right leads to Honeystreet Mill Café. Immediately after crossing the

---

The Sarsen Way now follows the White Horse Trail for 10.3km.

On the small green, at the junction in Alton Priors, there is a sarsen stone with a cut-out of the Alton Barnes White Horse on it.

The Church of St Mary the Virgin, which dates back to Saxon times, has a 16th-century tie-beamed and wind-braced roof, a Georgian gallery and some interesting monuments.

STAGE 3 – OVERTON HILL TO UPAVON

The Kennet and Avon Canal at Honeystreet

canal, turn right to join the towpath and turn right under the bridge. ▶

> The **Kennet and Avon Canal** opened in 1810 connecting Bristol to the River Thames at Reading. However, the opening of the Great Western Railway brought about its gradual decline. Fortunately, after years of neglect, the canal has been fully restored.

Follow the canal towpath for 3km. On the way, shortly before a bridge (123) over the canal, a signed path ('To Memorial') on the right gives access to a memorial commemorating the crew of an Albemarle Bomber that crashed nearby in 1944; to visit, go over the stile and turn left along the field edge parallel to the canal, then either retrace your steps or continue along the field edge and leave by a stile at the field corner (missing out bridge 123). At the next bridge (122) cross the canal to continue with the canal on your right. ▶ On reaching Ladies Bridge (120) turn right across the canal; 1.6km further along the towpath is Wilcot and the Golden Swan pub (campsite). Pass **Cocklebury Farm** and continue along the driveway to a road, opposite a sarsen boulder at **Swanborough Tump**.

Three hundred metres to the left along the canal is the Barge Inn (campsite); a further 2.8km is All Cannings and the Kings Arms (campsite).

To the south from bridge 122 via Woodborough is the Seven Stars pub at Bottlesford (accommodation, 1.7km each way).

43

The Kennet and Avon Canal at Woodborough Fields Bridge (122)

It was at **Swanborough Tump** that Alfred the Great met up with his brother, Ethelred, in AD871 on their way to fight the invading Danes and they swore that if either of them died in battle, the dead man's children would inherit the lands of their father, King Aethelwulf.

Cross the road, go over the stile and continue along the right-hand field margin, with **Frith Copse** on your right (alternatively, follow a permissive path passing to the right of the sarsen stone to reach the field and then continue along the right-hand edge). With great care, cross the railway and keep ahead, soon following a track (Dragon Lane) past houses to a junction with the main street in Manningford Bruce (the church is located away from the village – see later). Turn left for 60m, then turn right along the signed footpath following the left-hand field margin; continue straight on along the enclosed path, passing a thatched building. Keep ahead and then go along the track past the mill (left). Cross three footbridges over the River Avon and then go through a gate into a field where the path splits. Fork right across the field and go through a gate (joining the Pewsey Avon Trail); the left fork heads to the church at **Manningford Abbots**.

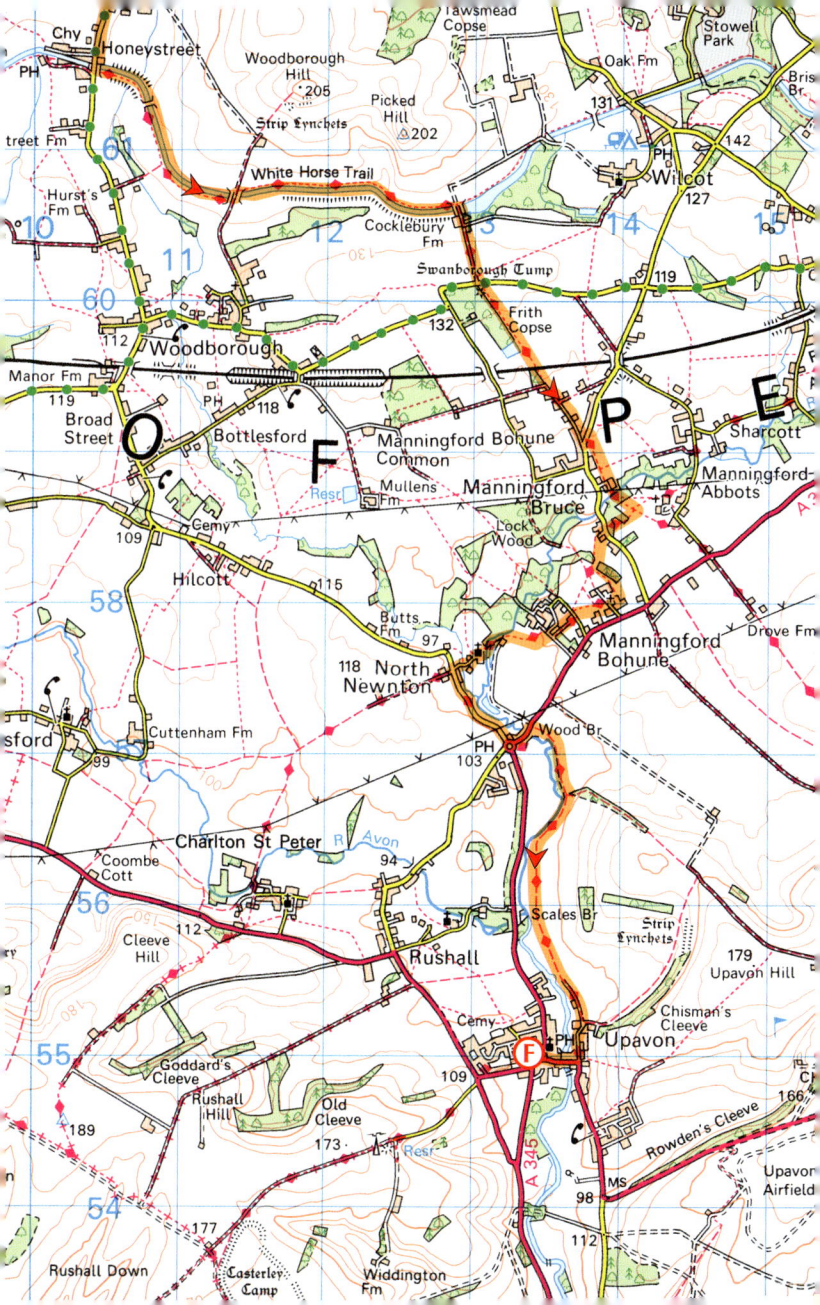

WALKING THE SARSEN WAY

There are three **Manningford villages**: Manningford Bruce; Manningford Abbots; and Manningford Bohune. The second part of the name refers to previous owners of the manors: Bohune from Humphrey de Bohun; Abbots was held by Hyde Abbey in Winchester until the Dissolution of the Monasteries in 1547; and Bruce, named after William de Breuse.

Pass through a boggy area (footbridges) and go through a gate. Bear half-right across the field, then through a gate and some trees. Cross straight over the minor road and continue along the enclosed path. Go through a gate, bear half-left across the field and leave through a gate. Keep ahead through the trees, crossing a footbridge and then go through a gate where the path splits.

Turn left (Pewsey Avon Trail) and follow the path with trees on your left to a gate. Continue alongside the brick wall (passing a gate) to the corner of the wall and bear right through the churchyard, passing to the right of St Peter's Church and leave through the gate. ◄ Cross the lane (manor house entrance to the right) and follow the enclosed path opposite. Cross a stile into the field and

> The small, late Saxon and early Norman Church of St Peter in Manningford Bruce, is worth a visit to see the colourful reredos (screen) in the apse and the stained-glass windows.

The colourful apse of St Peter's Church

follow the left-hand edge, then cross a stile on the far side to join a lane at **Mannigford Bohune**.

Turn left and then immediately turn right along a signed path (following the Pewsey Avon Trail and White Horse Trail). Keep ahead across the grass, keeping the buildings of the Manningford Bohune Business Park over to the right. Cross over the surfaced access track and keep ahead across the grass to a tarred drive. Turn right along this towards the large gate pillars (private), but before reaching them turn left along the grassy strip (hedge on right). Follow the path as it curves to the right to reach a stream at Manningford Trout Fishery. Cross the bridge, follow the gravel path and then bear right to follow the path alongside the stream, before crossing over to St James' Church in **North Newnton**. ▶ Pass the church and continue along the lane to a T-junction at Falkner's Farm and turn left; here the Sarsen Way leaves the White Horse Trail which goes straight on and now follows the Pewsey Avon Trail to Salisbury.

Follow the lane for 650m to a roundabout beside the Woodbridge Inn (campsite). Turn left (A345), immediately cross the road and then turn left following the verge towards Pewsey. Cross the River Avon at **Wood Bridge** and continue for 40m, then turn right along the bridleway for 550m to a junction. Fork right, later following a tarred lane past farm buildings and continuing along Vicarage Lane, past houses to a T-junction with the A342.

Turn right and cross the River Avon. ▶ Keep ahead to a junction (A342 and A345) and turn right to the small square in **Upavon**, beside a large sarsen stone; the stone was placed here to commemorate the Queen's Golden Jubilee.

> The **River Avon**, a classic chalk river that rises near Devizes and Pewsey before the two tributaries join near Upavon, is met and crossed many times while walking along the Sarsen Way. Upavon has a couple of pubs; the Antelope Inn (accommodation) and the Ship Inn, a village shop and bus services.

St James' Church in North Newnton, which dates from the 13th century, with later additions, is built on the site of an early 10th-century church.

After the first house on the right, a path gives access to the Church of St Mary the Virgin which dates from Norman times.

WALKING THE SARSEN WAY

REVERSE ROUTE – UPAVON TO OVERTON HILL

> From Upavon the route continues along the River Avon valley for a while before following the Kennet and Avon Canal to Honeystreet. Then it's off through the neighbouring hamlets of Alton Priors and Alton Barnes before heading up Walkers Hill, from where there are extensive views across the Vale of Pewsey. After passing the earthworks of the Wansdyke it's downhill to East Kennett and the stage end at Overton Hill.

In Upavon, stand with your back to the Antelope Inn and cross over the road, turn right and then left along Andover Road (A342 towards Everleigh). Continue across the River Avon to a junction and turn left along Vicarage Lane (later a track). At a bridleway junction keep left (straight on) along the valley to another bridleway junction. Keep left (field on right) and continue to the road (A345) at **Wood Bridge**. Turn left along the verge crossing the River Avon and just before the roundabout turn right across the road to the **Woodbridge Inn**.

Follow the road (Woodborough and Hilcott) just left of the pub for 650m to a junction at Falkner's Farm. Turn right along the lane to St James' Church in **North Newnton**; the Sarsen Way now follows the White Horse Trail to Walkers Hill, north of Alton Barnes. Pass just right of the church, cross the footbridge and continue on the path through the trees. Bear left along a track, cross over a stream and turn left, then immediately bear right along an enclosed path to a tarred drive. Turn right along this for 15m and then go left. Head across the grass, cross the access track and pass to the right of the buildings (business units), then along the enclosed path to a minor road in **Manningford Bohune**.

Turn left, then immediately right into a field where the path splits. Fork right, following the right-hand boundary, cross a stile on the right and continue along the enclosed path. Cross the lane and continue through the churchyard, passing to the left of St Peter's Church in **Manningford Bruce**. At the left-hand corner of the churchyard, follow the brick wall on your left (passing a gate). Go through a gate and follow the right-hand side of the field to a gate on the right and turn right through this.

Continue through the trees, cross a footbridge and through a gate. Bear half-left across the field to the far-left corner, go through a gate and follow the enclosed path. Cross the minor road and continue through the trees and a gate. Continue through the field to another gate and keep ahead through a boggy area (footbridges) to a third gate and a path junction. Bear left across the corner of the field and go through a gate. Continue through the trees crossing three footbridges, passing under the power lines and pass a mill (right). Where the track swings left go straight on through two gates and follow an enclosed path. On joining a minor road turn left to a junction and turn sharp right along Dragon Lane (later a track).

Ignore a track (path) to the right and when the byway turns to the left, fork right (straight on) along a path with trees on the left and a field to the right. With great care, cross over the railway line and continue along the path in the same direction, soon with Frith Copse on the left. Go over a stile beside the sarsen boulder at **Swanborough Tump** (alternatively, on nearing the field corner, fork left and follow a permissive path passing to the left of the sarsen boulder), cross the minor road and follow the track opposite towards **Cocklebury Farm** and go through a gate. Cross Ladies Bridge (120) over the Kennet and Avon Canal and turn left along the towpath; to the right is Wilcot (pub with accommodation; 1.6km).

At the next bridge (122; there is no 121) cross the canal and continue along the towpath (canal on right); to the south is Bottlesford (pub and accommodation; 1.7km each way). To visit the memorial commemorating the crew of an Albemarle Bomber that crashed nearby in 1944, shortly before the next bridge (123) turn left over a stile (signed 'To memorial') and continue parallel to the canal for 50m to the memorial; then retrace your steps or continue along the field edge to another stile and rejoin the towpath after bridge 123. Continue past bridge 123 towards **Honeystreet** and immediately after passing under the next bridge (124) turn sharp left to the road; 300m straight on along the towpath is the Barge Inn (campsite) and further on is All Cannings (pub and campsite; 2.8km each way).

Turn left along the road towards Alton Barnes, crossing the canal; a track on the left leads to Honeystreet Mill Café (the fields on the left of the road were once home to the former World War 2 RAF Alton Barnes). At the road junction turn right along the lane signposted to 'St Mary's Saxon Church' and at the end of a brick wall on the left go left through a turnstile and follow the cobbled path to a cross-junction mid-field and go straight on. To visit the church keep ahead, then exit back onto the lane, turn right and then right again on a path through the field to the cross-junction and turn right. Cross a couple of footbridges with turnstiles and continue along the cobbled path. Where this turns right to All Saint's Church in **Alton Priors**, keep ahead and go through another turnstile. Continue along the lane to a junction beside a sarsen stone with a carving of the Alton Barnes white horse on it. Turn left, then quickly right up the tarred track (bridleway) and keep ahead up to a minor road. Turn right up this for 75m, then turn left across the road and go through a gate. Follow the fence on the left and turn left through a gate. Follow the fence on the left to a gate on the left, do not go through this, but turn right up the wide path towards Walkers Hill.

Follow the path as its keeps left of the summit (although it's worth a detour to the top for the view and to visit Adam's Grave) to a col and path junction; here you can continue straight on following the Sarsen Way or opt to follow the Wansdyke and Alton Barnes White Horse route.

Wansdyke and Alton Barnes White Horse route
Turn left from the col and follow a path (White Horse Trail) as it contours round the hill for 500m to the **Alton Barnes White Horse** figure. Then continue contouring round **Milk Hill** (highest point in Wiltshire) and head northwards, with a fence over to the right. Go through a gate to a junction with a track; to the left is a view along the Wansdyke. Turn right and follow the bridleway alongside the earthwork for 1.6km, keeping left at a junction on the way to reach a cross-junction with the Sarsen Way and turn left (see sidebar below).

Reverse route continues
To continue along the Sarsen Way, keep ahead through a gate and continue downhill. Pass through another gate, continue through the field and go through a gate at the corner; across the road is a parking area and access to Knap Hill. Stay in the field and follow the byway up alongside the right-hand boundary through fields to a junction at the top with a bridleway, beside the earthworks of the Wansdyke. The alternative Wansdyke and Alton Barnes White Horse route joins from the left.

Keep ahead down the byway to a track junction; enjoying the views on the way which include Silbury Hill. Turn right, continue past farm buildings and then bear left (straight on) along a minor road through **East Kennett** to a junction. Fork right (West Overton direction), then fork left (straight on) at the next junction; the right-hand fork leads to West Overton. Cross the River Kennet and dogleg left then right, at a crossing bridleway; the optional Avebury loop turns left here (see Stage 2). To finish the stage, continue up the byway, passing the Sanctuary, and with great care, cross the A4 to car park at **Overton Hill**.

STAGE 4
Upavon to Netheravon

Start	Upavon High Street (SU 134 550)
Finish	Netheravon High Street (SU 147 490)
Distance	10.9km (7 miles)
Ascent	190m
Time	3¼hr
Maps	OS Explorer 130
Refreshments	Upavon, Longstreet and Netheravon
Public transport	Buses between Swindon and Salisbury stop at Upavon, Enford and Netheravon
Accommodation	Upavon, East Chisenbury (off-route) and Netheravon

A short stage from Upavon heads up to Casterley Camp on the edge of Salisbury Plain before dropping back down to the more tranquil surroundings of the River Avon, passing through the picturesque hamlets of Enford and Longstreet to arrive at Netheravon.

Stand facing the Antelope Inn on the High Street in Upavon and follow the main road just to the left of the pub. Keep right at a junction to follow the A342 (Devizes and Rushall). Shortly before the staggered cross-junction, fork left to pass a seat and then, with care, cross over the main road to take the minor road opposite signposted to Widdington. Follow this uphill for 2km to reach a small military building (Casterley Vedette) and track junction at the top, looking out over Salisbury Plain.

Salisbury Plain, an expansive area of chalk grassland, has been used by the Ministry of Defence since 1898 for training purposes. Some restricted areas are still used for live firing – you'll probably hear the sound of gun fire and see helicopters flying

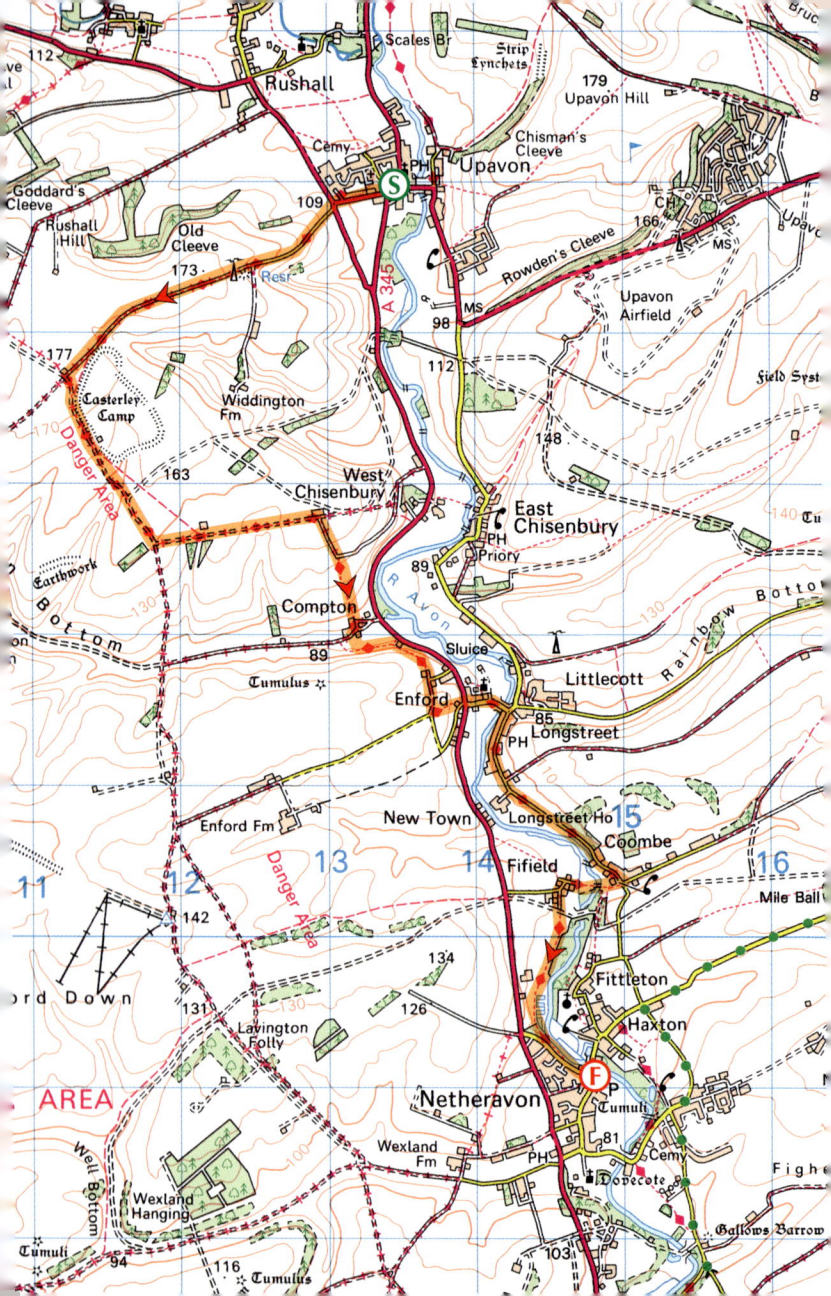

STAGE 4 – UPAVON TO NETHERAVON

overhead (obey all warning signs). The area is noted for its wildlife, including the nationally rare stone curlew and the reintroduced great bustard. The Casterley Camp earthworks are the remains of an Iron Age hill fort, although the area was also used during the Neolithic and Romano-British periods.

Turn left along the gravel track, passing a parking area, with **Casterley Camp** over to the left. On reaching a three-way junction (signposted 'A – Crossing') keep ahead to another three-way junction and turn left. Follow the track for 1.2km and once level with a building at West Chisenbury Farm, turn right down a surfaced track (byway). Where this curves left, keep ahead down between fences and keep ahead at the track junction beside a house to a tarred access track in **Compton**. Turn right along this through the farmyard of Compton Farm and go through a waymarked gate on the left. Keep ahead across the field and go through another gate at the corner. ▶ Follow the path (track) alongside the fence on your left and keep right of a thatched cottage.

Continue up the path, running parallel with the road (left). Go through a gate, keep ahead for 50m and turn

This is a permissive route between the two gates; the right of way follows the track for a further 100m to a stile on the left and then doubles-back across the field to the gate.

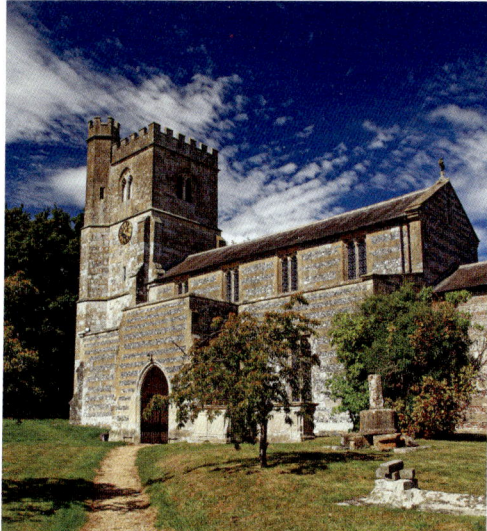

All Saints' Church at Enford

The River Avon at Enford

Enford was first mentioned in a Saxon charter dated AD934, when land was given to Winchester Cathedral by King Aethelstan; All Saints' Church dates from the Norman period.

right through a gate, then turn left (barns on right) along the track. At the junction keep ahead past the electricity substation (left) following the track (bridleway) up to a junction with a lane. Turn sharp left through a gate and head down across the field to another gate. Continue down through the trees (steps) to the A345; bus stop to the right. With care, cross straight over and follow the lane opposite down through **Enford**, passing All Saints' Church (left), then crossing the River Avon to a T-junction. ◄

STAGE 4 – UPAVON TO NETHERAVON

Turn right towards Netheravon and Coombe Lane. ▶ Follow the lane for 1.5km through Longstreet, home to some picturesque thatched buildings including the Swan Inn. Just before a junction in Coombe on the left, turn right along a surfaced path; spot the blue plaque on the wall, placed there in memory of two policemen who lost their lives on this spot in 1913. Keep ahead, crossing the footbridge over the River Avon.

The path soon becomes a lane at **Fifield**. Follow this as it curves left and, at the right-hand bend, fork left (straight on) down a track (path). Cross over the tarred military track and keep ahead across the field, soon following the trees on the left. Continue along the valley, following the left-hand boundary, and later keep ahead along the track towards Netheravon; over to the left is the River Avon with Fittleton's church beyond. Bear left (straight on) along the minor road (Mill Road), passing the Stonehenge Ales brewery, to a T-junction and the end of the stage in **Netheravon**; the next stage turns left towards Haxton. ▶

> **Netheravon** is home to All Saints' Church, parts of which date back to late Saxon times; there is also an early 18th-century dovecote near the church (private). The 20th-century author, Frank Sawyer, who designed the Pheasant Tail Nymph for fly fishing and wrote *Keeper of the Stream* and *Nymphs and the Trout*, spent much of his life in Netheravon as river keeper on the Avon. Just to the east is Netheravon Airfield, said to be the longest continuously operating airfield in the world, having been used by the Royal Flying Corps (forerunner of the Royal Air Force) since before World War 1.

Sidebar:

The lane to the left heads to East Chisenbury and the Red Lion pub (accommodation; 1.5km each way).

Seventy-five metres to the right along the High Street is a village shop and bus services; on the A345 is the Dog and Gun pub (accommodation).

Walking the Sarsen Way

REVERSE ROUTE – NETHERAVON TO UPAVON

> A short stage from Netheravon, following the River Avon through the picturesque hamlets of Longstreet and Enford. Then it's up to the Casterley Camp on the edge of Salisbury Plain before ending the stage at Upavon.

From the junction of Mill Road and the High Street in Netheravon head along Mill Road, soon passing the Stonehenge Ales brewery (right) and at the bus stop, just before Whitmarsh Close on the left, fork right on a track. Follow this parallel with the road for a while and then through fields, later with a wood on the right. Go through a gate and fork left (north) across the field. Cross straight over the tarred military track and continue to join a minor road in **Fifield**. Keep ahead (right) down past cottages and follow the road to the right. Soon fork left along an enclosed path and cross the footbridge over the River Avon. Keep ahead (spot the blue plaque on the wall on the left) to a road junction in Coombe. Turn left along the minor road for 1.6km to a junction in **Longstreet**, just after passing the Swan Inn. Turn left (Amesbury/Pewsey direction), crossing the River Avon again and then passing All Saints' Church in **Enford** to a junction with the A345.

With care cross straight over to the lane opposite and go up the steps on the right through the trees to a gate at the top. Continue up through the field and go through a gate to a lane. Turn sharp right along the track (bridleway) to a junction just after passing the electricity substation. Keep ahead past a barn (left) and go through a gate on the right. Turn left alongside the fence and then downhill with the A345 over to the right. Bear left behind a thatched cottage and follow the fence on the right.

Go through a gate and turn right to another gate. This is a permissive path; the right of way keeps ahead then turns sharp right along a track towards Compton Farm. Bear right through the farmyard, then left up past a house and follow the byway uphill to a surfaced track. Keep ahead to a T-junction in front of buildings at West Chisenbury Farm. Turn left to a T-junction and turn right along the track on the edge of Salisbury Plain. Keep ahead at a track junction and pass **Casterley Camp** (on your right) and parking area. At a four-way track junction, beside a small military building (Casterley Vedette), turn right along the tarred track down to the A342. With care cross straight over, bear left and then turn right down the road through **Upavon**. Keep left at the split to arrive at a junction beside the Antelope Inn on your left; to the left is a bus stop and village shop, with the Ship Inn on the opposite side of the road.

STAGE 5
Netheravon to Amesbury

Start	Netheravon High Street (SU 147 490)
Finish	Amesbury Church of St Mary and St Melor (SU 152 414)
Distance	10.6km (6½ miles); via Stonehenge 19.6km (12 miles)
Ascent	125m; via Stonehenge 270m
Time	3hr; via Stonehenge 5½hr
Maps	OS Explorer 130
Refreshments	Netheravon, Durrington, Bulford and Amesbury
Public transport	Buses between Swindon and Salisbury stop at Netheravon, Figheldean, Durrington, Larkhill, Bulford and Amesbury
Accommodation	Netheravon, Durrington, Bulford, Amesbury

From Netheravon the route continues along the Avon passing through picturesque hamlets on its way to Amesbury. An alternative loop takes walkers on a journey through history, passing Durrington Walls, Woodhenge and Stonehenge, as well as numerous burial mounds along the way, before heading to Amesbury.

From the junction of Mill Road and the High Street in Netheravon head north (turn left exiting from Mill Road), soon crossing the River Avon heading towards Haxton. Keep following the road round to the right, passing the small green with a tree and seat (left) and thatched cottages (right). Keep ahead past the turning for Lower Street (right) and after 50m, once level with the thatched cottage on the left, turn right along the fence-lined path. At the junction turn right, then left at the next junction. At a split, take the right-hand fork, keeping a small lake on your right, and continue along the tree-shaded path with the River Avon on the right to a minor road. ▶ Cross over and turn left to the left-hand bend and turn right, then go

To visit the church (and see the dovecote) turn right along the road, then left just before a three-way junction with a central tree and seat; beyond the junction is the A345 and the Dog and Gun pub (accommodation).

WALKING THE SARSEN WAY

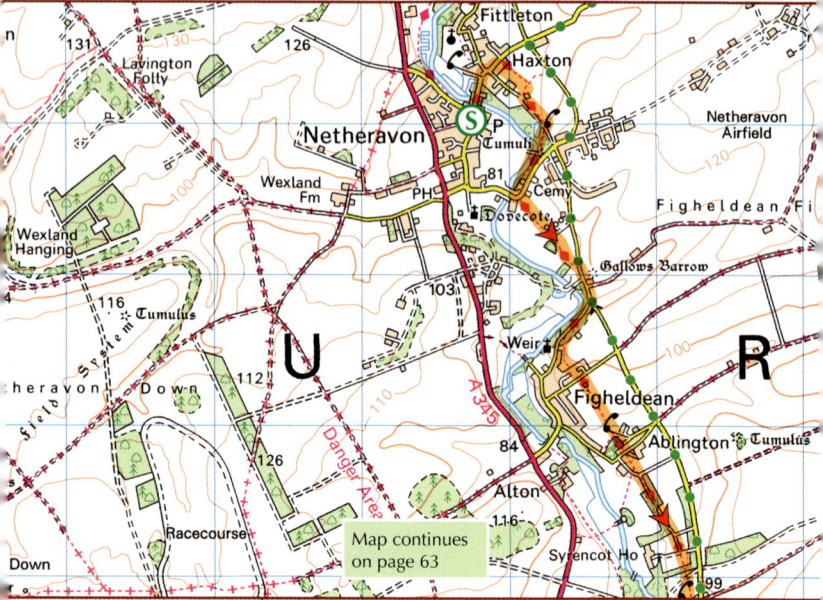

through a gate to the left of the Choulston Farm entrance (private).

Head south-east across the field, passing a sewage works (left) and small copse (right), then follow the field boundary to a gate. Turn right along the lane to a junction and fork right towards **Figheldean**. Follow the lane for 200m and once level with the church, turn left up through the trees; to visit the Church of St Michael and All Angels, continue along the lane for 65m to the War Memorial (right) and turn right to enter the churchyard, then retrace your steps and turn right. The church, which has a Norman tower and 15th-century Gothic nave, was first mentioned in a charter of Henry I.

Bear right alongside the fence on your left. Cross a track and continue past allotments and houses. Keep ahead across the minor road and pass just left of the village hall and recreation area. Continue straight on between fields,

STAGE 5 – NETHERAVON TO AMESBURY

then between houses and a wood. Pass the end of a lane (left) and keep ahead down to a minor road in **Ablington** opposite the entrance to Ablington Farm.

Turn right (south-west) for 10m and then go left through a gate. Keep ahead through the field, following the wall on the right at first. Leave via a stile, cross straight over a track and follow the tree-shaded track opposite. ▶ Later, cross a driveway (**Syrencot House**) and continue through trees to a track. Cross slightly to the right and continue past the marker post and across the grass to a tarred military track.

Cross straight over and continue through the field, then along the enclosed path between houses to a road at **Brigmerston**. Turn right and follow the road as it swings left and continue through **Milston** for 400m to a tarred track junction on the right, beside the Old Manor House, shortly before the church; here the Sarsen Way and the optional Stonehenge loop go separate ways (for the Stonehenge directions see the later section).

To stay with the Sarsen Way, keep ahead along the road, passing St Mary's Church on the right, which dates

For an alternative, permissive, route, continue along the lane for 50m, then turn left along the track to a stile on the left (main route) and turn right.

The route passes a thatched cottage after crossing the River Avon near Milston

from the 13th and 14th centuries, and follow the road as it curves left. At the next left bend, turn right past the metal railings and follow the surfaced path, crossing the River Avon. Turn left and soon re-cross the river. Continue to a lane and bear right up past two thatched cottages. As the lane curves left, turn right on a path through the trees.

Go through a gate and keep ahead through two more gates to enter a field. Bear right along the field edge and then along the track – later Church Lane – to a road (A3028) in **Bulford** beside the picturesque 12th-century St Leonard's Church with its squat tower; to the right across the road is the 17th-century Bulford Manor and 250m to the left is the Rose and Crown pub. ◀

> To the right along the A3028 is Durrington, with shops, cafés, bus connections and pubs, including the Stonehenge Inn (accommodation) and the Plough Inn.

Cross the A3028, go through the gate opposite and keep ahead over a footbridge and through the trees. Follow the right-hand field edge, cross a stile and turn left along the track to a junction. Turn right along the surfaced track, which soon curves left. At the entrance to Watergate Farm fishing lake, fork left up a narrow path through trees before bearing left (straight on) up the track. Pass under power lines and continue to a junction beside an electricity substation at **Ratfyn**.

Turn left along the tarred track (bridleway) and where this curves to the left, just after an entrance on the right, turn right on a narrower surfaced bridleway running parallel with the main road on your left. Cross the bridge over the A303 and continue along the bridleway, then turn right along Ratfyn Road to a junction (on the left, in a private garden, is a Bronze Age round barrow known as **Ratfyn Barrow**). Turn right through a gate to enter Lords Walk and head along the wide grassy path. Leave through a gate to the A345 and turn left. ◀ Continue along the pavement to a crossroads in **Amesbury**. Turn right along the High Street, passing the Amesbury History Centre (museum) on the right to arrive at the Church of St Mary and St Melor on the right, shortly before reaching the River Avon, marking the end of the stage; the town offers a range of services including shops, pubs, accommodation and bus connections.

> The alternative loop via Stonehenge rejoins the main route here from the right and continues along the A345.

AMESBURY

Amesbury, tucked in a bend of the River Avon to the east of Stonehenge, has a history stretching back 9000 years to the Mesolithic period. More recently Queen Elfreda founded an abbey here in AD979, and the present Norman Church of St Mary and St Melor originally formed the abbey church. To learn more about the town's history call in at the Amesbury History Centre (www.amesburyhistorycentre.org.uk). In 2002 the grave of a man dating back to the early Bronze Age was found in Amesbury. He became known as the 'Amesbury Archer' due to the number of flint arrowheads that were buried with him.

Overlooking Amesbury, from a defensive position to the north-west, are the tree-shrouded earthworks of Vespasian's Camp, a former Iron Age hill fort (although the area was used during the Neolithic and Mesolithic periods). Below this the Avenue – an ancient processional route to Stonehenge – sets out from the River Avon; recent excavations led to the discovery of a Neolithic henge and stone circle here. Just to the south-east is Boscombe Down Airfield, used for military aircraft research since 1939. And for all Beatles fans, the 'Fab Four' stayed at the Antrobus Arms Hotel in Amesbury in 1965 while filming scenes from their film *Help!*.

Stonehenge loop

At the junction beside the Old Manor House in **Milston**, shortly before the church, turn right along the tarred track (footpath). Continue between hedges and at the end turn right through a gate. Follow the right-hand field boundary to the far-right corner. Go through two gates 15m apart and then follow the enclosed path, crossing the footbridge over the River Avon to a road (B3085). Turn right along this up to a junction with the A345.

With care, cross straight over and follow the track (Martinbushes Road) up to a four-way junction. Turn left along the track, then keep ahead through the housing estate to a roundabout. Cross over and turn right (Larkhill direction) to a junction. ▶ Turn left along Wood Road to its end, then turn left along Fargo Road for 450m to a small gate on the left, ignoring all side roads off to the left.

Turn left through the gate and keep left (trees on left) to reach the earth embankment of **Durrington Walls**

To the left is Durrington offering shops, pubs, accommodation and bus connections.

WALKING THE SARSEN WAY

beside an information board (you can explore the earthworks). Turn right for 200m and then turn right again and leave through a small gate to rejoin the road. The onward route goes through the small gate opposite; however, before that, turn left along the road for 40m and then right through a gate to visit **Woodhenge**; on exiting, turn left along the road and then left through the small gate.

Durrington Walls is the site of a large Neolithic henge, around 500m in diameter; recent excavations found evidence for hundreds of houses dating from 2600BC. **Woodhenge**, which dates from 2300BC, originally consisted of six concentric upright timber circles that are now marked with concrete markers.

Having gone through the gate, follow the path diagonally right across the field for 80m, then fork half-right to a sarsen stone known as the Cuckoo Stone; originally a

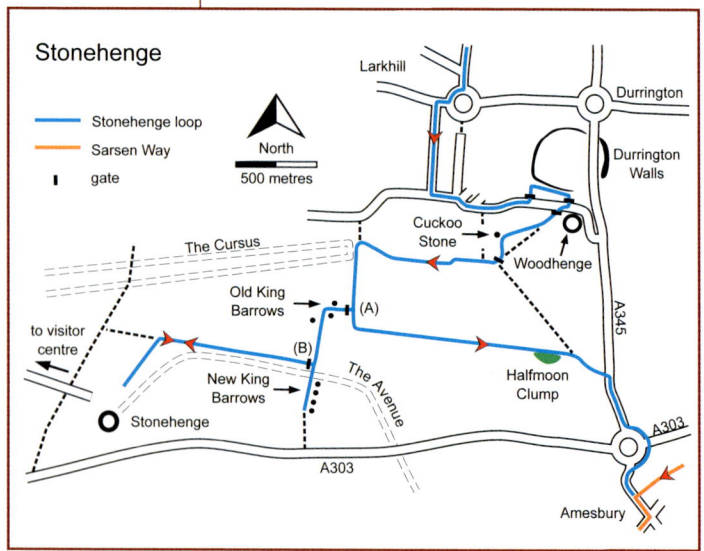

STAGE 5 – NETHERAVON TO AMESBURY

standing stone that has subsequently fallen over. Turn left and continue to a gate at the field corner. Keep ahead for a few metres and then turn right along the track-bed of the former Amesbury to Larkhill military railway. After 150m dogleg left-right and keep ahead, soon with houses on the right, to a cross-track junction at King Barrow Ridge; ahead is a view of **The Cursus**. ▶

Turn left along the track (bridleway) to a junction and turn right through a gate (A). Follow the track as it

Constructed in the Neolithic period, the Cursus consists of a narrow (100–150m wide) east-west aligned 2.8km-long rectangular bank and external ditch earthwork.

WALKING THE SARSEN WAY

It was through this area that the Avenue, the processional route that ran between the River Avon near Amesbury and Stonehenge, made its approach to the stones; the 4300-year-old earth banks can still be seen.

Concrete blocks mark the position of timber posts that once formed Woodhenge

bends left passing a copse at Old King Barrows, to reach a gate (B) on the right. The onward route turns right here; however, before that keep ahead for 300m to visit the New King Barrows, a well-preserved collection of early Bronze Age burial mounds to the left of the bridleway. Then retrace your steps to the gate (B) and turn left through it.

Keep ahead down across the field; over to the left is the magical outline of **Stonehenge**. Go through a gate in the dip and partway through the second field turn left up towards the stones for a closer view from outside the perimeter fence. ◄ Entry to Stonehenge is by timed ticket, book in advance at www.english-heritage.org.uk/stonehenge. To visit Stonehenge or the visitor centre, on reaching the perimeter fence turn right and follow the fence which is on your left, with Stonehenge beyond. On reaching a byway (track) turn left along it to a cross junction and follow the signs for the entrance; the visitor centre is 2km along the access road to the right.

64

The magical outline of Stonehenge

The area surrounding **Stonehenge** (designated a World Heritage Site along with Avebury) is littered with prehistoric remains, including Neolithic long barrows and over 300 Bronze Age round barrows. Stonehenge itself, which started out as a henge monument some 5000 years ago, was developed in several phases spanning several hundred years. The large sarsen stones came from the Marlborough Downs between Avebury and Marlborough, whereas the smaller 'bluestones' are from the Preseli Hills in south-west Wales, 250km away. As for its purpose, there are plenty of theories, but no one really knows.

Retrace your steps back through gates (B) and (A) to the junction visited earlier and turn right. Follow the track as it swings left, pass Halfmoon Clump (right) to a junction and bear right to the A345. Cross over and turn right along the pavement. Go through the pedestrian underpass at the A303 roundabout and continue southwards alongside the A345 (pavement) to the crossroads in **Amesbury**. Turn right along the High Street to the Church of St Mary and St Melor on the right.

Walking the Sarsen Way

REVERSE ROUTE – AMESBURY TO NETHERAVON

> From Amesbury the route heads north along the Avon passing through picturesque hamlets on its way to end the stage at Netheravon. An alternative loop takes walkers on a journey through history, passing Stonehenge, Woodhenge and Durrington Walls, as well as a number of burial mounds, before heading to Netheravon.

Stand with your back to the Church of St Mary and St Melor in Amesbury and turn left along the road. Keep left (straight on) at the junction following the High Street (passing the Amesbury History Centre) to a crossroads and turn left along Countess Road, crossing over at the traffic lights. Continue along the pavement for 150m, ignoring a cul de sac (Carleton Place) on the right, to reach the second track entrance on the right (Lords Walk); here the onward route goes right, while the optional Stonehenge loop goes straight on (see Stonehenge loop below).

Having turned right, go through the gate and continue along the wide grassy strip. Leave through a gate and turn left along Ratfyn Road for 180m. Turn left on a tarred path and follow this across the footbridge over the A303. Follow the route as it swings right to a junction and turn left along the lane to a cross-junction. Turn right along the track (electricity substation on right). Where the track bends left, fork right (straight on) down beside the trees and then bear right along the surfaced track. Just after the track curves right, turn left for 50m and turn right over a stile just before the house entrance. Follow the path along the field edge. Turn left over a footbridge and continue ahead to the A3028 in **Bulford**. Some 250m to the right is a pub; to the left is Durrington with shops, pubs, cafés, accommodation and bus services. Cross straight over and continue along Church Lane, passing St Leonard's Church on your left. Keep left (straight on) at the junction and where the lane curves left to a house, fork right (straight on) along the track. Keep ahead along the field edge, go through a gate and continue through two more gates and then through a wood to join a lane. Turn left down this past the thatched cottages to the end of the lane. Turn left, cross the River Avon and bear right, shortly recross the River Avon by turning right over another footbridge to a minor road. Turn left along this, passing the Church of St Mary in **Milston** and continue to a track junction on the left. The Stonehenge loop joins from the left.

Both routes now continue along the lane, later following it as it swings to the right. Just after the road on the left (The Croft) fork left along the enclosed path. Continue through the field and cross straight over the tarred military track. Keep ahead through the field to a track, dogleg right-left to continue along the path.

Northbound – Stage 5 – Amesbury to Netheravon

Pass some trees and cross the access drive to **Syrencot House** (left). Keep ahead along the track to a track junction and cross the stile opposite. Keep ahead, soon following a wall on the left and go through a gate to the road and turn right. An alternative permissive route turns left along the track rather than crossing the stile, then turns right along the road for 50m to rejoin the route that joins from the gate on the right.

Follow the road for 10m and once level with the entrance to Ablington Farm on the right, turn left along a path. Keep ahead with trees on the left, then straight on across the field and then past the village hall in **Figheldean**. Cross the lane and follow the enclosed path ahead between houses and past some allotments, keep right (straight on) at a junction and cross a track. As the path curves to the right, fork left down to the road and turn right along it. At the junction bear left for 175m and then fork left past a gate into a field. Keep ahead, passing a small copse (left) and a sewage works (right). On the far side go through a gate to join a minor road beside Choulston Farm.

Turn left for 40m and then turn right along a signed path through the trees, with the River Avon on the left. To visit the church in Netheravon continue along the road, then go left just before a three-way junction with a central tree and seat; beyond the junction is the A345 and a pub (accommodation). Later, follow the path as it curves left and continue to a track junction. Turn right and then left at the next junction, following a narrow path to a minor road at **Haxton**.

Turn left, ignore Lower Street on the left, then keep left at the junction, passing the small triangular-shaped green. Follow the road signed for Netheravon as it swings left and cross the River Avon to a junction in **Netheravon** (pub, shop and accommodation), marking the end of the stage; the next stage turns right along Mill Street.

Stonehenge loop

Keep ahead along the A345 to the roundabout and cross the A303 via the underpass. Then continue along the A345 (pavement) for 350m. Immediately after the third entrance road on the left, turn left across the road to pass a gate and follow the track (signposted Stonehenge 3½). Keep ahead past a pylon and follow the track as it bears left to pass Halfmoon Copse (left) and continue to a junction shortly after the right-hand bend.

Turn left and go through a gate (A), follow the track as it bends left passing a copse at Old King Barrows, to reach a gate (B) on the right. The onward route turns right; however, before that keep ahead for 300m to visit the New King Barrows, a well-preserved collection of early Bronze Age burial mounds to the left of the bridleway. Retrace your steps to the gate (B) and turn left through it. Keep ahead down across the field; over to the left is the magical outline of **Stonehenge**.

Sarsen Way passing through fields near Ablington

Go through a gate in the dip and partway through the second field turn left up towards the stones for a closer view from outside the perimeter fence. Entry to Stonehenge is by timed ticket, you can book in advance at www.english-heritage.org.uk/Stonehenge.

Retrace your steps back through gates (B) and (A) to the junction passed earlier and turn left to a junction; to the left is the Cursus. Turn right, later dogleg left-right and continue for 150m. Turn left for a few metres and go through a gate. Follow the left-hand edge of the field to the Cuckoo Stone (sarsen stone). Bear half-right across the meadow and leave through a gate to join a minor road; 40m to the right is the entrance to **Woodhenge**.

Go through the gate opposite and keep ahead to the earthworks of **Durrington Walls**. Turn left to the trees (information board) and turn left again, keeping the trees on the right. Leave through a gate and turn right along the minor road. Pass Fargo Close (right), then ignore three turnings on the right and at the fourth, turn right along Wood Road to a T-junction. Turn right to the roundabout, turn left and follow the road through the housing estate.

Keep ahead along the track to a cross-junction and turn right down the track (Martinbushes Road). With care, cross over the A345 and follow Hackthorne Road (B3085) for 300m. Turn left at the footpath sign and follow the enclosed path, crossing a footbridge over the River Avon on the way. Go through two gates 15m apart and follow the left-hand field boundary. Leave through a gate and follow the hedge-lined track to Church Road in **Milston** and turn left, now following the Sarsen Way again (see sidebar earlier); to the right is the Church of St Mary.

STAGE 6
Amesbury to Salisbury Cathedral

Start	Amesbury Church of St Mary and St Melor (SU 152 414)
Finish	Salisbury Cathedral (SU 142 296)
Distance	16.3km (10 miles)
Ascent	255m
Time	4½hr
Maps	OS Explorer 130
Refreshments	Amesbury, Great Durnford, Upper Woodford, Lower Woodford (off-route), Old Sarum and Salisbury
Public transport	Amesbury, Great Durnford, High Post and Old Sarum have bus links to Salisbury and Swindon; Salisbury has rail and bus connections
Accommodation	Amesbury, Great Durnford, Lake (off-route), High Post (off-route) and Salisbury

The final section of the Sarsen Way continues southwards from Amesbury passing the impressive earthworks of Old Sarum to finish at Salisbury Cathedral, one of Britain's finest medieval cathedrals that has stood for over 750 years. For those with time, it would be quite easy to spend a day in Salisbury exploring this historic city.

From the Church of St Mary and St Melor in Amesbury cross over Church Street and turn right along the pavement heading away from the centre. Cross the River Avon on the footbridge beside the 18th-century Queensberry Bridge and continue to the right-hand bend. Go straight on up Recreation Road to the entrance of **Bonnymead Park car park** and turn right along a footpath, passing to the right of the children's play area. Keep ahead, cross three footbridges over the River Avon and continue to a cross-junction near a house. Go straight on, rising gradually to a cross-track junction. Keep ahead (bridleway),

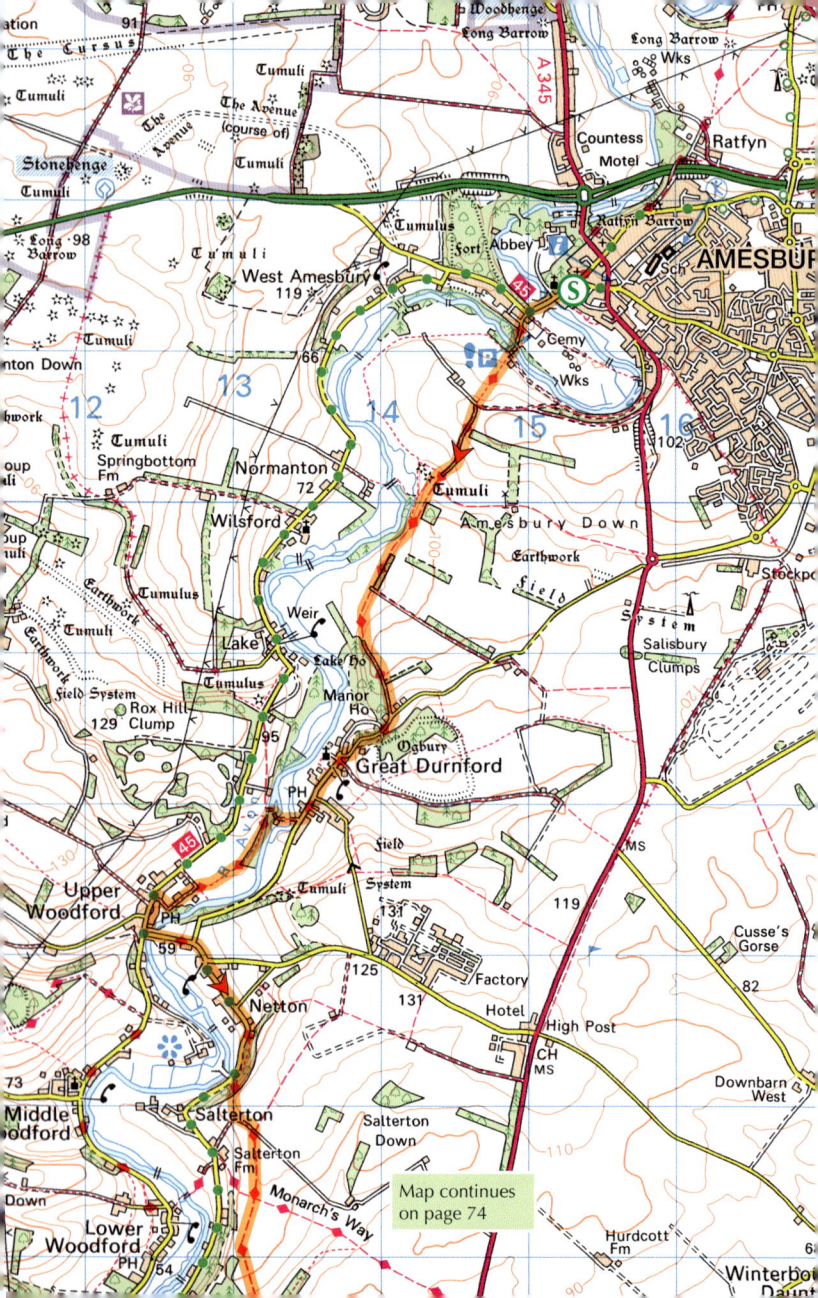

soon heading down to another junction, passing a gate and ignoring a bridleway to the left.

Continue along the track, rising slightly and pass to the right of a fenced plantation. Later head diagonally right to a gate in the field corner. Go through and continue along the enclosed track. Keep ahead at a cross-track and at the next track junction bear left, keeping Ham Wood on your right, and drop down to a lane beside a house. ▶ Turn right along the lane through **Great Durnford**, keeping left at the bottom of the hill, soon a lane on the right leads to the 11th-century St Andrew's Church. Continue through the village for 500m, passing a junction on the left and the Black Horse pub, to a gravel drive on the right. Turn right along this towards Durnford Mill. Follow the path across the footbridge to an island and then continue over another footbridge to a junction on the far side of the River Avon. ▶

Bear half-left up the slope to enter a field where the path splits and fork left to follow the left-hand boundary, later continuing between hedges to a track. Keep ahead

Queensberry Bridge crossing the River Avon at Amesbury

On the hill opposite is Ogbury Camp, a former Iron Age hill fort.

The bridleway to the right leads to Lake where there is accommodation; 1.1km each way.

Following the Sarsen Way towards Upper Woodford

The minor road at the second junction heads to the A345 at High Post and the Stones Hotel.

A long-distance route based on the escape route taken by King Charles II following his defeat by Cromwell in the final battle of the Civil Wars at Worcester in 1651.

at a crossing path and follow the track as it swings right to the main street in **Upper Woodford**. Turn left, keep ahead at the first junction and at the next junction, after passing the Bridge Inn, turn left across the River Avon.

Follow the road through **Netton** for 1.1km, keeping right at three junctions. ◀ Follow the road past a right-hand bend and 50m after the last house on the left, turn left through a gap into the trees. Continue up through the wood, then follow the right-hand field margin to a track at a bend with a seat. Down to the right, across the River Avon, is Lower Woodford and the Wheatsheaf pub (1.1km each way).

Turn left uphill for 150m to a bridleway junction and turn right, following the right-hand field margin. In the far corner, go through a gap and keep ahead through the trees, going straight on at the junction with the **Monarch's Way**. ◀ Head across the field and then down a track to a junction beside a thatched cottage (Keeper's Cottage). Keep ahead uphill, with trees on the right, then go past a wood (left) to reach an open field; ahead the earth ramparts of **Old Sarum** can be seen.

STAGE 6 – AMESBURY TO SALISBURY CATHEDRAL

Follow the track and drop down to buildings at Shepherds Corner. Continue straight on to a minor road (left leads to the Beehive park and ride and further on a shop). Cross over and take the fenced bridleway opposite for 400m, with the earthworks up to the right, and go through two gates to join the Old Sarum access road. ▶ Turn right up the access road to visit Old Sarum. On the way, pass a gate on the left beside the outer ramparts; this is the onward route to Salisbury.

For bus connections bear left down to the A345, cross over and turn right for 300m passing the Old Castle pub to the bus stop.

OLD SARUM

Ruins of an 11th-century Norman motte and bailey castle within the Iron Age earthworks at Old Sarum

Old Sarum, originally established as an Iron Age hill fort around 400BC, became the Roman town of Sorviodunum following the Roman invasion of AD43. Little is known about the site during the Saxon period. However, following the Norman Conquest of 1066, William the Conqueror quickly realised its potential and built the large motte within the earthworks, onto which was built a castle (now ruins). In the late 11th century a cathedral was built within the earthworks. However, its life was short as a new cathedral (the present one) was built in Salisbury, and the one at Old Sarum was later demolished. The castle and associated buildings were finally abandoned during the reign of Henry VIII, although Old Sarum lived on as one of the 'rotten boroughs' and continued to elect members of Parliament until 1832 (more information: www.english-heritage.org.uk/visit/places/old-sarum).

After visiting Old Sarum head back down the access road, passing through the outer rampart, and turn right through a gate (see earlier). Follow the main path (not

Walking the Sarsen Way

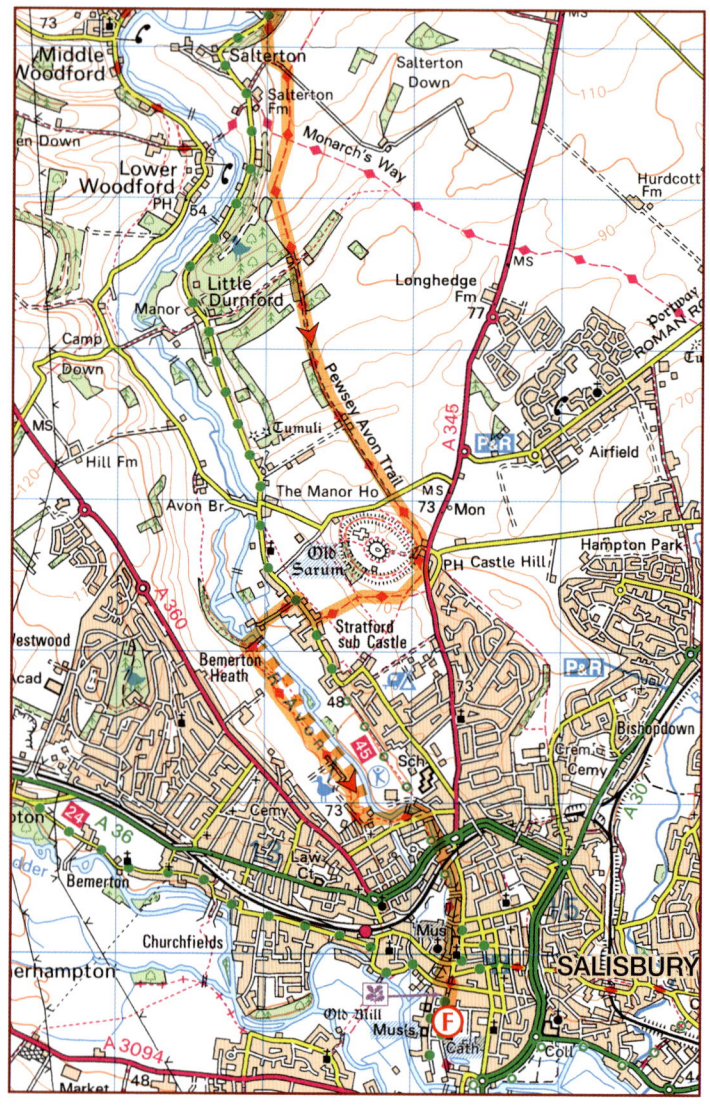

Little remains of the 11th- and 12th-century cathedral at Old Sarum

the one up the bank) as it curves left and go through another gate. Keep ahead and shortly before the A345 turn right on a path following the hedge on your right. Exit the field through a gate (signed Phillips Lane) and continue alongside the hedge on your right through the next field. Leave through a gate to a junction and fork left along an enclosed path. Keep ahead to join a minor road in **Stratford sub Castle**. Cross over and turn right along the pavement for 200m, then go left along Mill Lane. At the end, bear left (right is the entrance to Avonside House), and continue along the tarred path. Then cross the footbridge over the River Avon; here there is a choice of routes either following the Sarsen Way, or opting for a permissive riverside route.

Alternative riverside route

Immediately after crossing over the River Avon, turn left along a path. This veers away from the river for a while before continuing alongside the river, which is on the left. After passing a wetland area (with boardwalks), continue along the main riverside path (see below).

Main route continues

To continue along the Sarsen Way, after crossing the footbridge keep ahead to a cross-junction and turn left along the enclosed path, following it as it swings right and left; ahead is a view of Salisbury Cathedral. Go left and right at some allotments and continue along the path towards the centre of Salisbury. Keep ahead on the surfaced path as it curves left through the riverside park (this area, which includes wetland areas and boardwalks, is part of the Salisbury River Park Scheme designed to reduce flooding); on approaching the river the alternative riverside route rejoins from the left. Continue along the riverside path, keeping the River Avon on your left and ignoring a bridge on the left.

Cross over Ashley Road and continue along the riverside route, passing under the A36 and then the railway. Shortly, turn left across a footbridge (the River Avon splits here; the Sarsen Way follows the left-hand channel) and continue along the riverside route (water on your left), crossing some access roads and ignoring footbridges. At The Maltings, where the main path swings left, fork right (straight on) through the brick archway (signed for Cathedral, Museums and Riverside Walk). Pass the Bishops Mill (pub) and cross a footbridge to join Bridge Street opposite the King's Head Inn. ◀

The railway station is to the right along Fisherton Street (700m); for the bus station turn left, follow the road left along Minster Street, then right on Blue Boar Row and left along Queens Street (450m).

Cross over Bridge Street (zebra crossing), turn right and then left just before the bridge to continue along the riverside path (King's Head on your left, river on your right) to join Crane Street. ◀ To continue with the Sarsen Way turn left along Crane Street to a crossroads and turn right along the High Street. Pass through the ancient gateway and continue past Choristers Square; to the right is the 18th-century Mompesson House, a perfect example of Queen Anne architecture (www.nationaltrust.org.uk/visit/wiltshire/mompesson-house). Keep ahead to North Walk and continue to the west door of **Salisbury Cathedral** marking the end of the Sarsen Way; this is also the starting point of the Cranborne Droves Way and the Avon Valley Path.

The Cranborne Droves Way (described later in this guidebook) heads west along this road having left the cathedral.

STAGE 6 – AMESBURY TO SALISBURY CATHEDRAL

SALISBURY

The early 13th-century Salisbury Cathedral was built over a short period of time using a single architectural style known as Early English Gothic. This makes it unique among medieval English cathedrals, which typically display several architectural styles. The cathedral, which houses many treasures, also has Britain's tallest spire at 123m; climb the 332 steps to the foot of the spire for a great view (www.salisburycathedral.org.uk).

The city of Salisbury offers a full range of facilities and numerous interesting sites. Within the Close, in addition to the impressive cathedral, there is Arundells, once the home of former prime minister Sir Edward Heath (www.arundells.org); the Salisbury Museum, which traces several thousand years of history (www.salisburymuseum.org.uk); and The Rifles Berkshire and Wiltshire Museum (www.thewardrobe.org.uk).

The impressive west façade of the medieval Salisbury Cathedral marking the southern end of the Sarsen Way and the northern end of the Cranborne Droves Way

WALKING THE SARSEN WAY

REVERSE ROUTE – SALISBURY CATHEDRAL TO AMESBURY

> The first section of the Sarsen Way starts from Salisbury Cathedral, one of Britain's finest medieval cathedrals that has stood for over 750 years; if you have the time to spare there is plenty to explore in the historic city of Salisbury. The route leaves behind Salisbury to arrive at the impressive earthworks of Old Sarum before continuing to Amesbury.

Stand facing the west façade of Salisbury Cathedral and turn left. Continue through Choristers Square; to the left is Mompesson House. Keep ahead through the ancient gateway to a crossroads and turn left along Crane Street. The Sarsen Way now follows the Pewsey Avon Trail all the way to North Newnton. Just before the bridge turn right (the Cranborne Droves Way goes straight on). Follow the surfaced path to Bridge Street beside the King's Head Inn on your right. Turn right, then left across the road (zebra crossing) and cross the footbridge to the right of the Bishop's Mill pub. Go through the archway and keep ahead along the riverside path with the water on your right, crossing some access roads. Follow the path as it bears left to cross a footbridge, then turn right and continue alongside the River Avon (on your right), soon passing under the railway bridge and then the A36.

On reaching Ashley Road, cross over and continue alongside the river, ignoring a bridge on the right. Keep to the main surfaced path as it curves right through the riverside park (this area, with wetland areas and boardwalks, forms part of the Salisbury River Park Scheme designed to help reduce flooding). Keep left to pass some allotments, then bear left and right and continue along the enclosed path to a crossing track at a four-way junction and turn right. Alternatively, on reaching the play area on your left, fork right and follow a riverside path upstream, keeping the river on your right to a junction with a crossing track and turn right. Cross the River Avon and keep ahead, following Mill Lane to a T-junction in **Stratford sub Castle**.

Turn right along Stratford Road for 200m, then turn left across the road and follow the track (bridleway) beside a thatched cottage signposted 'Old Sarum ½ mile'. Keep ahead along the enclosed route and where this bends left go through a gate to enter a field. Follow the left-hand hedge, go through a gate and continue through the next field following the left-hand boundary to a T-junction with a tarred path; to the right is the A345 (pub and bus stop). Turn left and bear right passing through a gate to join the access road for **Old Sarum** which is to your left. The Sarsen Way turns right and just before the farm, turns left through two gates. Follow the fenced bridleway and later cross the minor road; to the right is the Beehive park and ride and further on is a shop. Continue down the track to a

NORTHBOUTH – STAGE 6 – SALISBURY CATHEDRAL TO AMESBURY

Keeper's Cottage between Netton and Old Sarum

junction beside a cottage and go straight on uphill. Keep ahead as the route heads down to a crossing path in a dip beside Keeper's Cottage. Go straight on uphill, keeping right (straight on) at the Y-junction. Keep ahead through the large field, then through a copse, crossing the **Monarch's Way**. Continue along the bridleway on the left side of the field to a junction with a track.

Turn left down this track for 150m to a junction on the right beside a seat (down to the left, across the River Avon, is Lower Woodford and the Wheatsheaf pub; 1.1km each way). Bear right, following the fence on the left to the corner and keep ahead down through the trees to a minor road. Turn right along this heading through **Netton**, keeping left at three junctions to arrive at a T-junction after crossing the River Avon. Turn right passing the Bridge Inn (left) in **Upper Woodford** and after 200m turn right along a signed footpath following the gravel drive. Continue along the enclosed track, keep ahead at a junction at Woodford Green to enter a field. Keep ahead, later with a wood on the right to a junction. The bridleway ahead leads to Lake where there is accommodation; 1.1km each way. Turn right and cross a footbridge over the River Avon, then cross another

WALKING THE SARSEN WAY

The peaceful River Avon at Upper Woodford

footbridge beside Durnford Mill and continue along the drive to a junction with a road at **Great Durnford**.

Turn left along this, passing the Black Horse pub (left); later a track to the left leads to St Andrew's Church. Continue along the road as it bends right and rises. On reaching a house (Fairwood House) on the left, fork left up the track (bridleway) through Ham Wood. Fork right, leaving the wood, and keep ahead at a crossing track. Continue along the enclosed track and through a gate. The route splits, fork right (track) following the field edge and keep left of a plantation. Head downhill and go through a gate. Keep ahead up along the track and go straight on at a crossing track. Head down to a cross-path junction beside a house and keep ahead over footbridges crossing the River Avon at Ham Hatches. Continue along the track, passing to the left of a play area (Bonnymead Park) and continue along the access road (Recreation Road) to a junction. Bear right (straight on) along the road, soon crossing the River Avon on a footbridge beside Queensbury Bridge to arrive at the Church of St Mary and St Melor on your left in **Amesbury**.

THE CRANBORNE DROVES WAY

The Ox Drove looking east above Ebbesbourne Wake (Stage 1)

STAGE 1
Salisbury Cathedral to Cow Down Hill

Start	Salisbury Cathedral (SU 142 296)
Finish	Minor road at Cow Down Hill (SU 023 216)
Distance	17.3km (10¾ miles)
Ascent	325m
Time	5hr
Maps	OS Explorer 130
Refreshments	Salisbury; Coombe Bissett, Bishopstone and Broad Chalke (all off-route)
Public transport	Salisbury has rail and bus connections; Coombe Bissett, Bishopstone, Broad Chalke and Bowerchalke (all off-route) have bus links to Salisbury and Shaftesbury
Accommodation	Salisbury; Broad Chalke (off-route); Bowerchalke (off-route)

From Salisbury's magnificent cathedral the route heads out through Harnham Water Meadows crossing the River Nadder on the way before following old trackways to Stratford Tony. From here the route continues through the undulating downland landscape of Cranborne Chase to Cow Down Hill; on the way the route joins up with the Ox Drove, an old drovers' route, that is followed all the way to Win Green. For information about Salisbury, see Stage 6 of the Sarsen Way.

Stand facing the west façade of Salisbury Cathedral and turn left. Continue through Choristers Square (Mompesson House is off to the left) and pass through the ancient gateway to a crossroads. Turn left along Crane Street and continue over Crane Bridge crossing the River Avon. ◄

The Sarsen Way joins from the right, just before the bridge; shortly on the left there is a car park and toilets.

Continue along Crane Bridge Road as it swings left and keep left (straight on) at the mini-roundabout following Mill Road. Where this curves right, fork left along the surfaced path signed 'Harnham via Town Path'. Cross the

Salisbury Cathedral viewed from Harnham Water Meadows

footbridge over the River Nadder and follow the raised path through Harnham Water Meadows with a view of Salisbury Cathedral over to the left, later crossing a weir and then passing the Old Mill Hotel. Keep ahead to a junction with Middle Street in Harnham.

Harnham Water Meadows, located at the confluence of the River Avon and the River Nadder, date back to the 17th century. Some of the meadows are still flooded (or 'drowned') in the winter to provide early grass for sheep grazing, just as they have been for over 300 years.

Turn right along Middle Street for 600m and follow the road as it curves left and becomes Upper Street. Keep ahead to a junction with Netherhampton Road (A3094). Cross straight over and continue along Carrion Pond Drove (bridleway) opposite for 300m to a junction, with the disused West Harnham chalk pit (quarry) ahead.

Turn right, up through trees to enter a field and follow the field edge ahead as it curves left. At the field corner, turn right and continue between fields to the far

WALKING THE SARSEN WAY

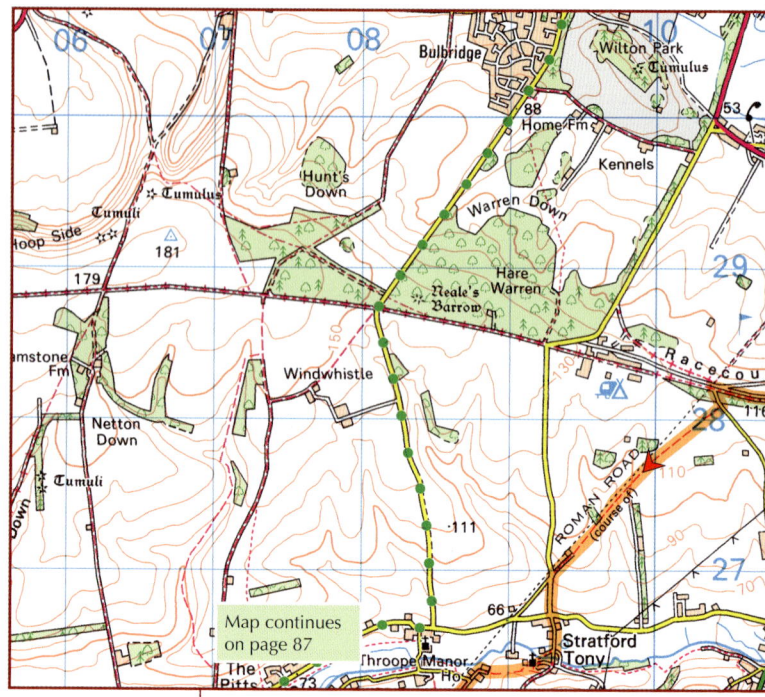

The Roman road, known as Ackling Dyke, ran between Old Sarum and Badbury Rings (Vindocladia).

side. Turn left and follow the track uphill, where it turns right, go straight on passing under the power lines to a T-junction with a track (byway).

Turn right along the byway (Old Shaftesbury Drove – an old ridge-top route between Salisbury and Shaftesbury) for 1km to a junction on the left; **Salisbury Racecourse** is on your right. Turn sharp left along the track (Drove Lane) for 150m then turn right through a gate entrance (bridleway). Continue along the left-hand field edge, now following the former Roman road. ◄ Keep ahead along the track (stand of trees on your left) and where the track turns left, go straight on following the left-hand field edge. Keep ahead through the trees and continue down to a minor road.

STAGE 1 – SALISBURY CATHEDRAL TO COW DOWN HILL

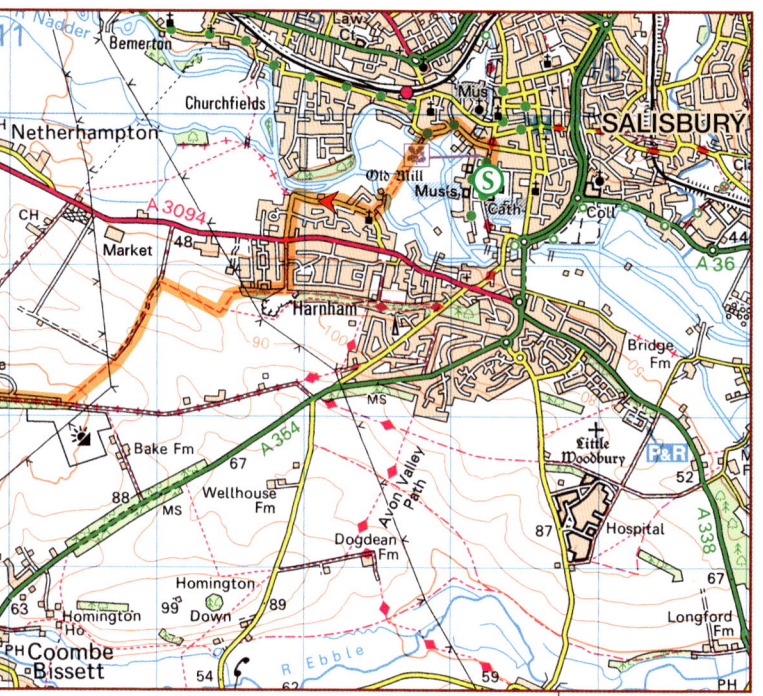

Turn left towards Stratford Tony, keeping left (straight on) at the junction to a crossroads at Manor Farm. Cross straight over and continue through **Stratford Tony** to a junction. ▶ Take the right-hand fork, signposted 'Historic Church', with a wall and house on your right. Cross a footbridge over the River Ebble and then keep right up the track towards the church (accessed through the hedge gap on the right).

The hamlet of **Stratford Tony** is home to the Church of St Mary and St Lawrence which dates from the 13th century; the church is now cared for by the Churches Conservation Trust. The Roman road between Salisbury and Blandford forded the River

The left-hand fork (path) heads to Coombe Bissett, home to the Fox and Goose pub, shop and bus links (1.7km each way).

WALKING THE SARSEN WAY

Ebble hereabouts, giving rise to the name 'strat' (or street) and 'ford'; the second part of the name is from Ralph de Toni, who was given the manor of Stratford following the Norman Conquest. The River Ebble, a chalk stream that rises near Alvediston, joins the River Avon at Bodenham, near Nunton.

STAGE 1 – SALISBURY CATHEDRAL TO COW DOWN HILL

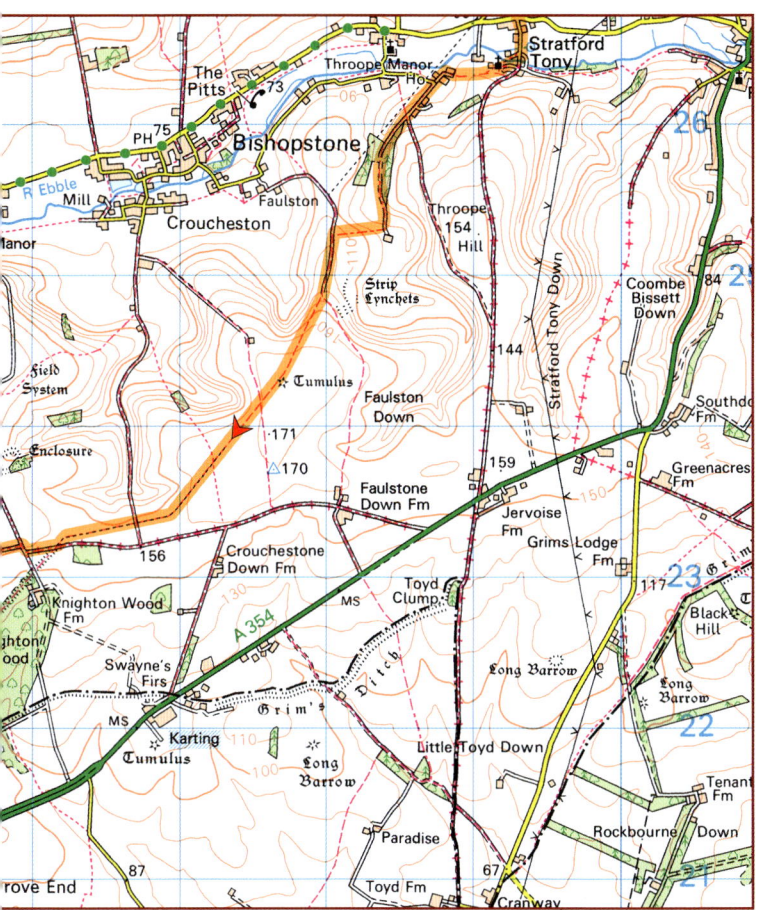

Bear left alongside the hedge to a T-junction, turn right and immediately fork left (redundant stile) across the meadow to the far corner. Go through a hedge gap (redundant stile) and turn right along the enclosed bridleway to an oval-shaped green at Throope Farm. Go to the far side of the green and turn left along the surfaced drive, passing **Throope Manor** on your right, to a three-way junction.

Keep left (straight on) along the concrete track, soon passing some barns on your left, to a junction. Keep ahead past the trees and just before some buildings at Throope Bottom Cottages, turn right uphill. Go through a gate at the top to a junction with a track (bridleway) and turn left. ◀ Follow the bridleway uphill – now following the Roman road again – and pass a gate to a split junction.

Fork right (straight on) still following the Roman road uphill. Near the top, before the trees and scrub on the right end and before the track swings left, fork right into a field and turn left to follow the boundary on your left for 50m. Then fork right across the field to the opposite side, passing to the right of a covered reservoir. Pass through a hedge gap to a junction with a bridleway. ◀ Keep ahead across the corner of the field (coombe to the right). Go through into the next field and continue in the same direction. Keep ahead at a crossing path (soon with another coombe to the right) and then bear right to a junction with a hedge-lined track (bridleway) known as Croucheston Drove. Keep ahead across the field, later

The bridleway to the right leads down to Bishopstone, home to the White Hart pub, bus links and a 17th-century dovecote (1.7km each way).

The bridleway to the right, Croucheston Hollow (track), leads down to Croucheston and Bishopstone (2.3km each way).

The Ox Drove looking east above Ebbesbourne Wake

STAGE 1 – SALISBURY CATHEDRAL TO COW DOWN HILL

bear left and go through a hedge gap to join a tree-shaded track (byway), which is the **Ox Drove**, and turn right. ▶

The **Ox Drove**, an ancient trackway, or drovers' route for driving livestock (sheep or cattle) on foot to market, follows a more southerly route than the Old Shaftesbury Drove visited earlier. No one knows how old the route is, it might be Anglo-Saxon or medieval, but could be much older. Its route, which crosses a number of parishes, and is only metalled in parts, is now followed by the Cranborne Droves Way for 15km to Win Green.

At the T-junction with a tarred track, turn right for 30m to a junction and turn left. Continue along the track to a crossing bridleway; to the right leads down to Broad Chalke (3.2km each way) and the next path on the right, shortly before **Hut & Lodge Farm** leads to Middleton Down Nature Reserve.

Broad Chalke, the largest village in the Chalke Valley which stretches from Salisbury to Shaftesbury, is home to the 13th-century All Saints'

If the field is under crop, follow the left-hand boundary along two sides of the field to regain the bridleway and turn left through the hedge gap, then turn right along the byway.

Queens Head pub, Broad Chalke (off-route)

A path to the right leads down the east side of Marleycombe Hill to Bowerchalke (accommodation and bus links; 2km each way); the next path on the right also leads down to Bowerchalke.

To the south (off-route) is Martin Down National Nature Reserve, an area of chalk grassland with the Bokerley Ditch (or Dyke), a linear Bronze Age earthwork, along its western edge.

The Ox Drove and Cranborne Droves Way heading towards Hut & Lodge Farm

Church. There is also a pub, the Queens Head (accommodation), a village shop/café (The Hub) and bus links. **Middleton Down Nature Reserve** is an area of traditional chalk downland, home to several species of orchid and butterfly (access via a gate at SU 046 228).

Continue along the byway, passing Lodge Farmhouse on your left, to a junction with a minor road. Cross straight over and continue along the track (byway), soon passing the open access woodland of Vernditch Chase on your left. ◄ Keep ahead to arrive at a parking area and minor road on **Cow Down Hill** marking the end of the stage (to continue with Stage 2 cross straight over and continue westwards). ◄

Bowerchalke, tucked below the chalk downland of Marleycombe Hill, is home to the Holy Trinity Church, which dates from the 13th century. Sir William Golding, author and Nobel Prize winner, lived in Bowerchalke for many years; both he and his wife, Ann, are buried in the churchyard. Other notable residents included the World War 1 poet Siegfried Sassoon and Professor James Lovelock; Lovelock is best known for the Gaia hypothesis, which suggested that the Earth functions as a self-regulating system. The rather short River Chalke rises nearby and joins the River Ebble near Broad Chalke.

COW DOWN HILL TO SALISBURY CATHEDRAL

> From Cow Down Hill the route continues along the Ox Drove through the undulating downland landscape of Cranborne Chase to arrive at Stratford Tony. Then it briefly follows the course of a Roman Road before heading through the Harnham Water Meadows crossing the River Nadder on the way to end at Salisbury's magnificent cathedral.

From the minor road at Cow Down Hill head east along the track (byway) past the stand of trees and small parking area. A path to the left leads over Marleycombe Hill and then down to Bowerchalke (accommodation and bus links; 2km each way), the next path on the left also leads down to Bowerchalke. Continue along the track with Verndich Chase on the right. Cross straight over the minor road and continue, soon passing Lodge Farmhouse and then the buildings of **Hut & Lodge Farm**; just after the farm a path on the left gives access to Middleton Down Nature Reserve. Ignore a restricted byway on the right and then keep ahead at a crossing bridleway. The bridleway to the left (north) leads down to Broad Chalke (pub, accommodation, shop/café and bus links; 3.2km each way).

At the next junction, turn right along the tarred track for 30m, then turn left (byway) and follow the track to a bridleway marker at a hedge gap on the left. Turn left here into the field and bear half right to the middle of the field and then turn right to a hedge gap. If the field is under crop, follow the right-hand field edge along two sides of the field to the hedge gap instead. Cross straight over Croucheston Drove (bridleway) and keep ahead through the next field for 200m, then bear half-left and continue. Keep ahead at a crossing path, pass the field boundary and keep ahead, with a coombe to the left.

Go through a gate in the hedge and continue in the same direction through the field, passing left of a covered reservoir. On reaching the far side turn left following the field edge for 50m to the field corner. Turn right through the gap and then turn left down the track (Roman Road). Keep ahead as a bridleway (Faulstone Drive) joins from the right and continue down the track for 400m to waymark. The bridleway straight on leads to Bishopstone (pub and bus links; 1.7km each way). Turn right through a gate and continue down to a junction with a track near some buildings (Throope Bottom Cottages) and turn left.

Follow the track for 1.2km past trees and then some barns (right) to a three-way junction; the lane to the left leads to the Church of St John at Bishopstone (500m each way). Keep ahead past the buildings of **Throope Farm** (right) and turn right past the oval-shaped green in front of some houses. Continue along the

Walking the Sarsen Way

enclosed bridleway. At a hedge gap (redundant stile), fork left on a path across the small meadow to a track at **Stratford Tony**. Turn right and immediately turn left down a track past the Church of St Mary & St Lawrence on your left (accessed through the hedge gap).

Keep ahead across the footbridge over the River Ebble, continue alongside a house and wall to a junction. A path to the right (east) leads to Coombe Bissett (pub, shop and bus links; 1.7km each way). Turn left along the lane to the crossroads and go straight on following the minor road opposite. Just after the point where a road joins from the left, turn right onto a track (bridleway) and go through the gate. Continue along the track (Roman Road) heading north-east gently uphill. Keep ahead along the right-hand field edge and then straight on along a track that joins from the right. Keep ahead past a small copse, ignoring a track off to the left and continue alongside the right-hand field edge to a lane (Drove Lane).

Turn left along this to a track junction and turn right along the byway (Old Shaftesbury Drove), with **Salisbury Racecourse** on the left. Continue for 1.1km and turn left (bridleway) just before a pylon on the right. Continue downhill for 850m, joining a track on the way. Then turn right between fields and at the top, turn left and follow the track downhill, ignoring a path off to the right. Keep to the bridleway as it swings right and continues to descend through a wooded area, passing under the power lines on the way, near a disused quarry.

At the junction turn left to the A3094 in **Harnham**. Cross straight over and continue along Upper Street, follow this as it bends to the right to become Middle Street. Keep ahead ignoring all side turnings until you reach the Old Mill House (left). Immediately after the house, turn left along the lane (Town Path). Keep ahead past the Old Mill Hotel and follow the tarred path as it crosses a weir and continues through Harnham Water Meadows, enjoying the views of Salisbury Cathedral over to the right on the way.

Cross a footbridge over the River Nadder and bear right along Mill Road in Salisbury. At the mini roundabout, keep right along Crane Bridge Road (car park and toilets on the right) as it soon bends right and crosses the River Avon. The path to the left is the Sarsen Way heading north after starting at Salisbury Cathedral. Continue along Crane Street to a crossroads and turn right along the High Street. Pass through the ancient gateway and go straight on along the edge of Choristers Square (Mompesson House over to the right). Then keep ahead along the tarred path to arrive at the magnificent west façade of **Salisbury Cathedral**, marking the end of the Cranborne Droves Way and the start of the Sarsen Way.

STAGE 2

Cow Down Hill to Win Green or Shaftesbury

Start	Minor road at Cow Down Hill (SU 023 216)
Finish	Win Green (ST 924 206)
Alternative finish	St Peter's Church, Shaftesbury (ST 862 229)
Distance	10.7km (6¾ miles); to Shaftesbury 19.2km (12 miles)
Ascent	205m; to Shaftesbury 380m
Time	3hr; to Shaftesbury 5½hr
Maps	OS Explorer 118
Refreshments	Ebbesbourne Wake, Berwick St John and Tollard Royal (all off-route); Ludwell and Shaftesbury (Shaftesbury extension)
Public transport	Ebbesbourne Wake, Alvediston and Berwick St John (all off-route) have bus links to Salisbury and Shaftesbury; Shaftesbury has good bus links including to Salisbury (railway station)
Accommodation	Bowerchalke (off-route); Woodminton (off-route camping); Ludwell; Tollard Royal (off-route) and Shaftesbury (Shaftesbury extension)

The final stage continues westwards along the downs following the Ox Drove, an old drovers' route, with some lovely views to the north, gradually increasing in height to end the Cranborne Droves Way at Win Green. After soaking up the wonderful views from this lofty location you can continue on an optional route along the Wessex Ridgeway and Hardy Way to end at Shaftesbury, home to the well-known Gold Hill.

Cross straight over the minor road at Cow Down Hill and head westwards along the hedge-lined track – the Ox Drove – to a minor road junction. Keep ahead along the minor road, signposted for Ebbesbourne Wake and Shaftesbury, for 1.7km with views to the right over **Woodminton Down**. At the cross-junction, where the road turns right downhill, go straight on along the track

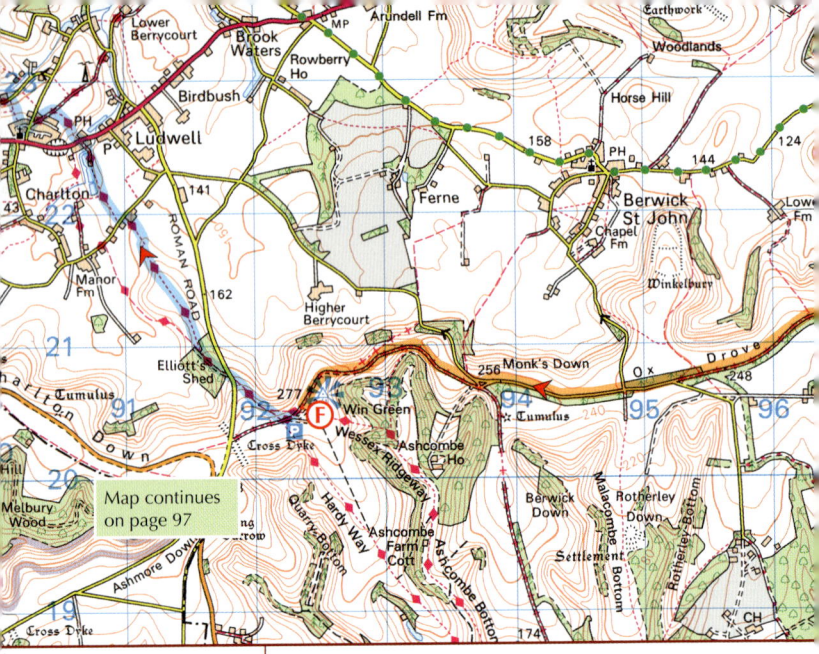

The road to the right heads down to Ebbesbourne Wake, home to the Horseshoe Inn, bus links and the church of St John the Baptist (2.7km each way).

The road to the right heads down to Berwick St John, home to the Talbot Inn, St John's Church and bus links (1.9km each way).

(byway). ◀ Keep ahead along the track (byway) for 1.3km to a junction, with a barn to the left; the track to the right (Elcombe Hollow) leads down to Alvediston (1.9km each way).

Alvediston is home to the Church of St Mary and bus links. In the churchyard lies the tomb of Sir Antony Eden, UK Prime Minister (1955–57); Eden lived at Alvediston Manor from 1968 until his death in 1977.

Continue straight on (in the field on the right is the Wermere, a large depression, or dew pond), pass Bigley Barn and go straight on at a junction. Follow the tree-shaded track up a rise and keep ahead; the second bridleway on the right leads to Winkelbury Hill crowned by the earthworks of an Iron Age hillfort (900m each way). On joining a minor road bear right (straight on) along this for 1.5km, keeping ahead at a road junction with views to the right over **Monk's Down**. ◀

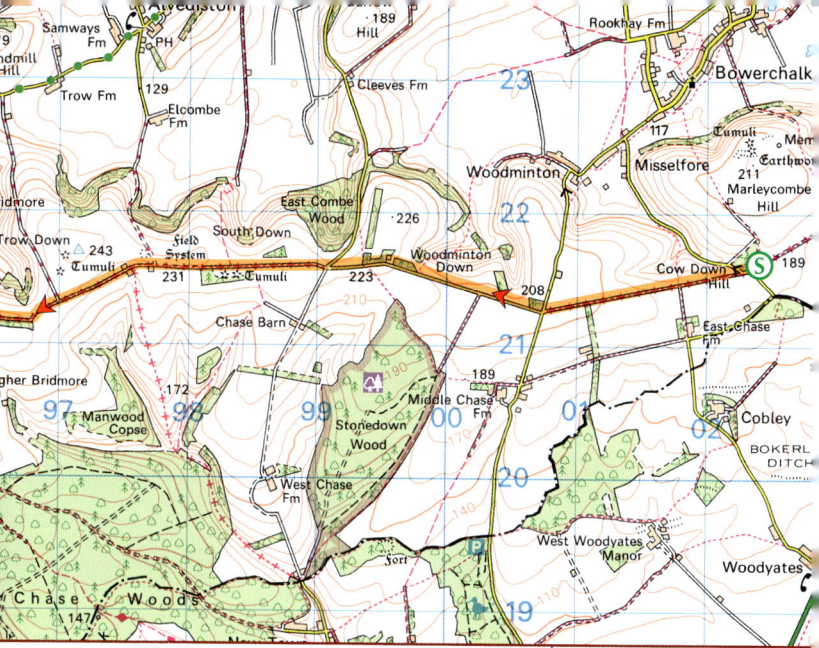

As the road starts to descend (before the right-hand bend), fork left on a track for 25m to a junction and bear right. ▶ Keep right at the split and follow the track (Ox Drove); soon **Win Green** comes into view. Follow the track as it curves left, with views to the right including Ferne House. As the track starts to rise, fork left through a small gate (National Trust) and head up to the copse on Win Green. Continue past the trig point and toposcope down to the **car park**, marking the end of the Cranborne Droves Way.

> **Win Green** at 277m is the highest point in the Cranborne Chase National Landscape and affords a great view that includes Shaftesbury (west-north-west), Blackmore Vale (west) and the Needles on the Isle of Wight (south-east); the toposcope gives more details.

The byway to the left leads down to Tollard Royal, home to the King John Inn (accommodation) and the 13th-century Church of St Peter ad Vincula (3km each way).

The beech copse crowning Win Green – marking the end or start of the Cranborne Droves Way

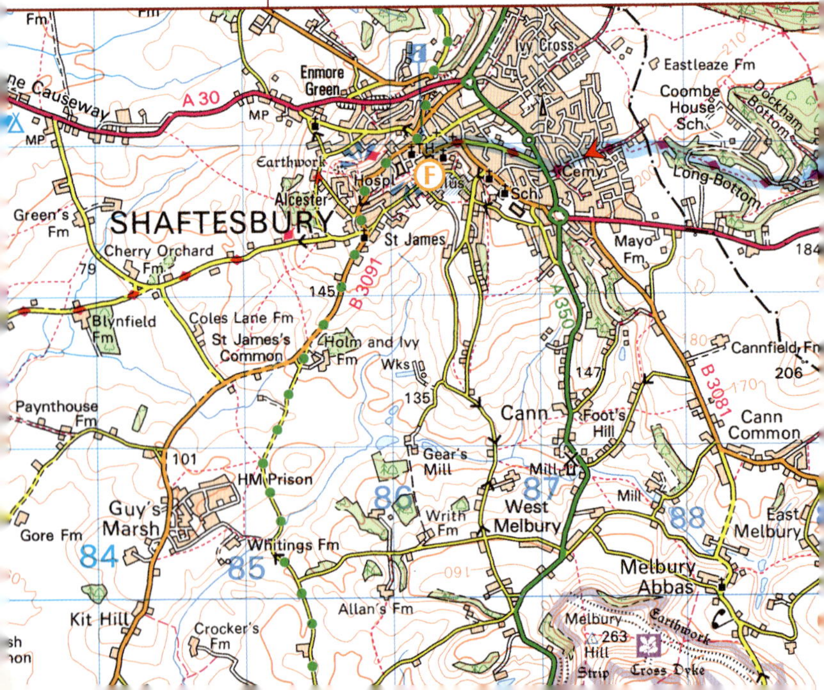

STAGE 2 – COW DOWN HILL TO WIN GREEN OR SHAFTESBURY

Extension to Shaftesbury (8.5km; 185m ascent)

From the car park head along the access track for 50m and turn right through a gate. Follow the bridleway (Hardy Way and Wessex Ridgeway) downhill, with a fence on the right. Later, bear left over to the trees on the left side of the field and cross a stile beside a gate. With care, turn right down the minor road for 50m and then turn left across it. ▶ Follow the bridleway down through the trees of **Elliott's Shed** to a junction and fork right (Wessex Ridgeway) to a stile. Continue across the field to a stile on the far side. Follow the right-hand boundary down through three fields. Leave the third field over a stile and keep ahead, with Peckons Hill dairy on your right. Turn left along the minor road for 50m and then turn right along a narrow, enclosed path. Turn left over a stile and then bear half-right through the narrow field to the far end. Cross a stile beside the gate, just right of a building and keep ahead along the track, with the

This minor road lies on the line of a Roman road that ran from Badbury Rings (Vindocladia) heading north through Ludwell towards Bath (Aquae Sulis).

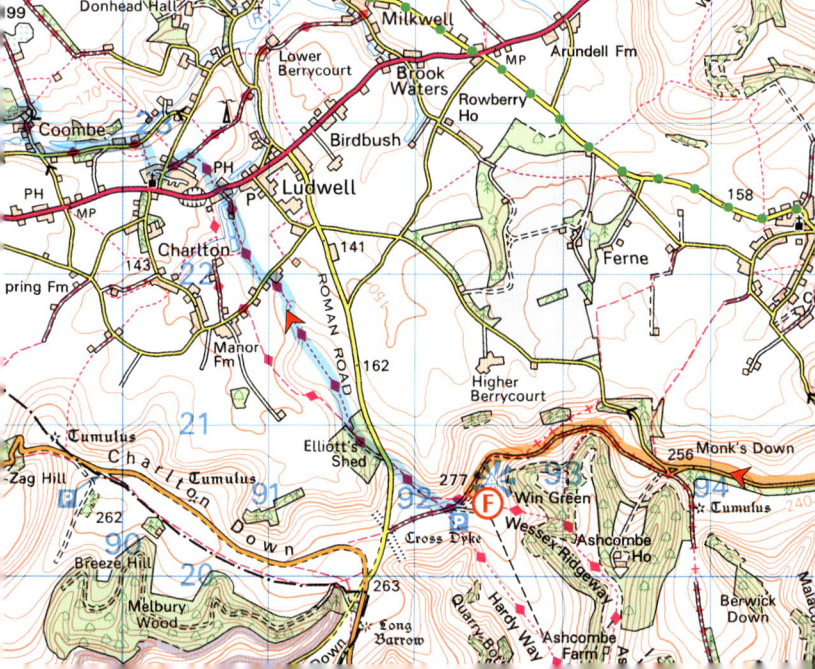

watercress beds on your left, to the A30 in **Ludwell** opposite the Grove Arms pub (accommodation).

Cross over and turn left for 25m, then turn right through a gate and follow the path as it curves right up to the top right corner. Turn right over a stile and bear left up through the field to another stile. Turn left along the track to a school (right) and keep right along the road to a T-junction, now following the Hardy Way. Turn left and shortly before reaching the A30 turn right across the road and take the track (bridleway) just to the right of the entrance gate for the Church of St John the Baptist. Follow the enclosed path and keep ahead across the residential street. Go through a gate, follow the left-hand field boundary and go through two gates. Head steeply down through the field to a gate.

Turn left along the minor road to a cross-junction and turn right. Follow the lane for 350m, later heading up past houses at Middle Coombe as the lane swings right and left to arrive at a crossing footpath (fingerpost). Turn left through the left-hand of two gates and follow the path along the left-hand edge of the trees (Morgan's Hanging). Cross stiles either side of a field and continue through the next field passing left of two large trees. Cross the stile beside the gate and keep ahead to a lane with a large house opposite. Turn left, ignore a track (path) to the right and shortly turn right through a gate.

Follow the enclosed path, go through a gate, then down some steps and turn right along the lane. Follow this as it curves left round Well Cottage (left) and go through a gate. Continue through the trees, then a gate and continue along the middle of a long, narrow meadow – **Long Bottom** – to the far end. Go through a gate and bear right up to a tarred drive. Turn left along this for 25m and then turn right over a stile. Continue through the trees (pond on left), then up the enclosed path to a kissing gate. Keep ahead, cross a stile and follow the right-hand field edge, with farm buildings on the right, passing from Wiltshire into Dorset. Go through a gate and follow the enclosed path past buildings. Go through a kissing gate, turn left along Mampitts Lane and Mampitts Road. Where this curves left, go straight on along the path and cross the road (A350) at the traffic lights.

Turn right, ignore St Rumbold's Road on the left and then turn left along Coppice Street to a four-way junction. Keep ahead along the High Street (B3091) to reach St Peter's Church on the left, marking the end of the route to **Shaftesbury**. Opposite the church is a bus stop for services to Salisbury (train services); just beyond the church is the Town Hall and the access route to Gold Hill (both on the left); ahead along Park Walk are the abbey ruins and museum.

SHAFTESBURY

Gold Hill in Shaftesbury

The market town of Shaftesbury in Dorset is probably best-known as the home of Gold Hill. This steep, picturesque, cobbled street, was the setting for the well-known 1973 'Boy on a Bike' TV advert for Hovis Bread. However, there is more to explore, including St Peter's Church that was built in the 15th century. Nearby is the Shaftesbury Abbey Museum and Gardens (www.shaftesburyabbey.org.uk). Founded in the late 9th century by Alfred the Great, Shaftesbury Abbey was the first great abbey for women and it became an important and wealthy Benedictine nunnery. All that came to an abrupt end during Henry VIII's Dissolution of the Monasteries in 1539. Today, only the foundations survive along with items recovered in archaeological excavations that are now displayed in the museum.

Walking the Sarsen Way

REVERSE ROUTE – SHAFTESBURY OR WIN GREEN TO COW DOWN HILL

Alternative start from Shaftesbury

> An alternative start from Shaftesbury, home to the well-known Gold Hill, follows the Hardy Way and Wessex Ridgeway up to Win Green.

Stand with your back to St Peter's Church in Shaftesbury and turn right along the High Street. At the junction, go straight on along Coppice Street to a T-junction. Turn right and after crossing St Rumbold's Street, turn left and cross the road (A350) at the traffic lights. Keep ahead on the tarred path and then straight on along Mampitts Road for 500m.

At the end of the houses, turn right through a kissing gate and follow the enclosed path. Go through a gate and continue along the left-hand field edge (farm buildings on left). Cross a stile and keep ahead to a path junction. Go through the right-hand of two kissing gates and follow the enclosed path downhill. Continue through the trees (pond on right) to a tarred drive. Turn left for 25m and then turn right down through the trees and go through a gate. Bear left through the long, narrow meadow – **Long Bottom** – and leave through a gate. Keep ahead through the trees and follow the track as it curves right past Well Cottage. Continue along the lane and turn left up some steps, go through a gate and follow the enclosed path downhill. Go through a gate to a minor road and turn left. On drawing level with a stone house on the left, turn right. Cross the stile beside the gate and continue through the field passing just right of two large trees. Cross stiles either side of a field and continue along the right-hand edge of a wood. Go through a gate and turn right down the lane passing through Middle Coombe and then up to a cross-junction.

Turn left for 750m and on reaching a thatched cottage on the left, fork right through a gate. Bear right up through the field, go through two gates and follow the right-hand field edge to a gate. Keep ahead between houses, cross the residential road and continue straight on along the enclosed path to reach a road in **Ludwell**, beside the church on the right. Turn left, ignore a road to right and then one to the left, and then turn right along Coronation Drive. Continue to a school on your left and fork left along the track. Turn right over a stile and head down through the field. Cross a stile and turn left down through another field to a gate in the bottom left corner.

Turn left alongside the A30 and once level with the Grove Arms pub, turn right across the road. Follow the track opposite between houses, soon with

Northbound – Stage 2 – Shaftesbury or Win Green to Cow Down Hill

watercress beds on your right. At a small building, fork left over a stile beside a gate and continue through the field. Go over a stile on the left side of the field and turn right along the enclosed path to a minor road. Turn left for 35m and after passing a house (right), turn right on a signed path. Cross the stile, with Peckons Hill dairy on the left, and continue along the left-hand boundary up through three fields, separated by stiles. At the top of the third field cross another stile and continue straight on through the long field towards the trees of **Elliot's Shed**. Keep ahead through the wood; the Hardy Way joins from the right.

Exit the trees, with care cross over the minor road and turn right to follow this uphill for 50m. Then turn left at a field entrance and cross the stile beside the gate. Bear half-right uphill, soon with a fence on your left. At the top left corner go through a gate and turn left along the access track to the **Win Green car park** on the right, the starting point of the Cranborne Droves Way.

The Cranborne Droves Way from Win Green

> This stage sets out from the lofty heights of Win Green, soon following the Ox Drove – an old drover's route – to end at Cow Dow Hill.

From the top of the car park, go through the gate and head up to the copse crowning **Win Green**, passing the toposcope and trig point. Continue in the same direction down to a gate; the Cranborne Droves Way now follows the Ox Drove for 15km. Keep ahead along the track (byway) to a junction and bear half-left to a minor road. The byway bears right and heads down to Tollard Royal (pub and accommodation; 3km each way). Keep ahead (bear right) along this, keeping straight on at a junction; the road to the left heads down to Berwick St John (pub and bus links; 1.9km each way).

Where the road curves to the right, fork left (straight on) along the tree-shaded track (byway). The first bridleway on the left leads to Winkelbury Hill and its hillfort. Follow the track downhill and continue straight on to pass Bigley Barn; at the next junction, a track – Elcombe Hollow – leads down to Alvediston (bus links; 1.9km each way).

Continue eastwards, ignoring side routes to join a minor road at a cross-junction. The road to the left heads down to Ebbesbourne Wake (pub and bus links; 2.7km each way). Go straight on along the road passing **Woodminton Down** to a cross-junction. Keep ahead along the track (byway) for 1.6km to a minor road at **Cow Down Hill**; the road to the left leads to Bowerchalke.

APPENDIX A
Useful contacts

The Friends of the Ridgeway
www.ridgewayfriends.org.uk

Wiltshire Ramblers
www.wiltsswindonramblers.org.uk

Tourist information
Visit Wiltshire
01722 342860
www.visitwiltshire.co.uk

Swindon Tourist Information
tel 01793 466454

Salisbury Tourist Information Centre
tel 01722 342860

Shaftesbury Tourist Information Centre
tel 01747 853514

Public transport information

Train enquiries
National Rail
tel 08457 484950
www.nationalrail.co.uk

Bus timetables
Traveline
tel 0871 2002233
www.traveline.info

Salisbury Reds
tel 01202 338 420
www.salisburyreds.co.uk

Other contacts
English Heritage
tel 0870 333 1181
www.english-heritage.org.uk

National Trust
tel 0844 800 1895
www.nationaltrust.org.uk

North Wessex Downs National Landscape
www.northwessexdowns.org.uk

Cranborne Chase National Landscape
www.cranbornechase.org.uk

Wiltshire Wildlife Trust
tel 01380 725670
www.wiltshirewildlife.org

For sick, injured or distressed animals and birds
RSPCA tel 0300 1234 999
www.rspca.org.uk

APPENDIX B
Selected accommodation near the route

Stage	Location	Name	Type	Facilities	Tel	Website
1	Swindon	Numerous choices				
1	Coate (Swindon)	The Sun Inn	Pub	Food, accommodation	01793 523292	www.suninn-swindon.co.uk
1	Coate (Swindon)	Holiday Inn	Hotel	Food, accommodation	0333 3209353	www.ihg.com
1	Chiseldon	Chiseldon House Hotel	Hotel	Food, accommodation	01793 741010	www.chiseldonhouse.com
2	Winterbourne Monkton (2.9km off route)	The New Inn and Elderbrook House	B&B	Food, accommodation	01672 539793	www.elderbrookhouse.com
2	Avebury (on Avebury loop)	Avebury Lodge B&B	B&B	Food, accommodation	01672 539023	www.aveburylodge.co.uk
2	Avebury Trusloe (700m off Avebury loop)	Aveburylife Bed & Breakfast	B&B	Food, accommodation	01672 539644	www.aveburylife.com
2	East Kennett	The Old Forge B&B	B&B	Food, accommodation	01672 861686	
3	Honeystreet	The Barge Inn	Pub, campsite	Food, accommodation	Campsite: 07917 407522 Pub: 01672 851222	www.thebargeinnhoneystreet.uk

WALKING THE SARSEN WAY

Stage	Location	Name	Type	Facilities	Tel	Website
3	Honeystreet	Well Cottage B&B	B&B	Food, accommodation	01672 851655	
3	All Cannings (3.1km off-route)	The Kings Arms	Campsite	Food, accommodation	01380 860328	www.kingsarms allcannings.co.uk
3	Bottlesford (1.7km off-route)	The Seven Stars	Pub	Food, accommodation	01672 851325	www.thesevenstarsinn.co.uk
3	Wilcot (1.6km off-route)	The Golden Swan	Campsite	Food, accommodation	01672 562289	www.thegoldenswan.co.uk
3	North Newnton	The Woodbridge Inn	Campsite	Food, accommodation	01980 630367	www.woodbridgeinn.co.uk
3	Upavon	The Antelope	Pub	Food, accommodation	01980 630025	www.antelopeupavon.co.uk
4	East Chisenbury (1.5km off-route)	Red Lion and Troutbeck Guest House	B&B	Food, accommodation	01980 671124	www.eastchisenbury.com
4	Netheravon	Dog and Gun	Pub	Food, accommodation	01980 670838	www.dogandgun netheravon.co.uk
5	Durrington	Stonehenge Inn	Pub	Food, accommodation	01722 433186	www.thestonehengeinn.co.uk
5	Bulford	Rose and Crown	Pub	Food, accommodation	01980 638633	www.roseandcrown bulford.co.uk

Appendix B – Selected accommodation near the route

Stage	Location	Name	Type	Facilities	Tel	Website
5	Amesbury	Antrobus Arms Hotel	Hotel	Food, accommodation	01980 623163	www.antrobushotel.co.uk
5	Amesbury	Fairlawn House	Hotel	Food, accommodation	01980 622103	www.alittleplace.co.uk
5	Amesbury	The George Hotel	Hotel	Food, accommodation	01980 622108	www.george-amesbury.co.uk
5	Amesbury	Travelodge Amesbury Stonehenge	Hotel	Food, accommodation	0871 9846218	www.travelodge.co.uk
5	Great Dunford	The Black Horse	Pub	Food, accommodation	01722 782270 (undergoing redevelopment at the time of publication; the name and tel number may change)	
5	Lake (1.1km off route)	Finch Cottage B&B	Accommodation	Food, accommodation	07837 025545	www.finchcottage.co.uk
6	High Post (2.3km off-route)	The Stones Hotel	Hotel	Food, accommodation	01722 782020	www.thestoneshotel.co.uk
6	Salisbury	Numerous choices including a youth hostel and campsite				

WALKING THE SARSEN WAY

Stage	Location	Name	Type	Facilities	Tel	Website
1	Broad Chalke (3.2km off-route)	Queens Head	Pub	Food, accommodation	01722 780344	www.queenshead broadchalke.co.uk
1	Bowerchalke (2km off-route)	Impstone House B&B and shepherd's hut	B&B	Accommodation	01722 781077	www.chalkevalley shepherdshut.co.uk
2	Woodminton (1.2km off-route)	Chalke Valley Camping	Campsite	Accommodation	01722 780881	www.chalkevalley camping.co.uk
2	Berwick St John (1.9km off-route)	Talbot Inn	Pub	Food, accommodation	01747 828222	www.talbotinmber wickstjohn.co.uk
2	Tollard Royal (3km off route)	King John Inn	Pub	Food, accommodation	01752 516207	www.butcombe.com/ the-king-john-inn-wiltshire
2	Ludwell	Grove Arms	Pub	Food, accommodation	01747 828811	www.grovearms-ludwell.co.uk
2	Shaftesbury	Numerous choices including campsites				

APPENDIX C
Further reading

Salisbury, history around us by John Chandler (Hobnob Press, 2020)

Prehistoric Wiltshire An Illustrated Guide by Bob Clarke (Amberley Publishing, 2011)

Pewsey Avon Trail by Chris Cole (Hobnob Press, 2010)

The North Wessex Downs by Steve Davison (Robert Hale Ltd, 2013)

The Making of Prehistoric Wiltshire by David Field and David McOmish (Amberley Publishing, 2017)

Stonehenge: A Brief History by Mike Parker Pearson (Bloomsbury Academic, 2023)

Avebury: The biography of a landscape by Joshua Pollard and Andrew Reynolds (The History Press, 2002)

Stonehenge: The Story of a Sacred Landscape by Francis Pryor (Pegasus Books, 2018)

APPENDIX D
Stage facilities planner

The Sarsen Way

Stage	Place	Walking time	Cum. stage time	Distance (km)
1	**Coate Water**	**0hr**	**0hr**	**0km**
1	*Swindon*			*0km (+4km)*
1	Chiseldon	1hr	1hr	4km
2	**Barbury Castle**	**3¼hr**	**3¼hr**	**11.3km**
2	*Broad Hinton*			*15km (+3.1km)*
2	*Winterbourne Bassett*			*15km (+2.5km)*
2	*Winterbourne Monkton*			*17km (+2.9km)*
2	*Avebury*			*19.1km (+2.6km)*
3	**Overton Hill**	**6hr**	**2¾hr**	**21.9km**
3	East Kennett	6¼hr	¼hr	22.7km
3	Honeystreet	8½hr	2½hr	29.8km
3	*All Cannings*			*29.8km (+3.1km)*
3	*Bottlesford*			*29.8km (1.7km)*
3	*Wilcot*			*32.9km (+1.6km)*
3	North Newnton	10½hr	4½hr	37.5km
4	**Upavon**	**11¼hr**	**5¼hr**	**41.2km**
4	Enford	13¼hr	2hr	48.2km
4	*East Chisenbury*			*48.2km (+1.5km)*
4	Longstreet	13½hr	2¼hr	48.7km

Appendix D – Stage facilities planner

- ⊙ hotel/B&B/guesthouse
- ▲ campsite
- 🍴 refreshments
- ⊕ grocery shop
- ✪ outdoor shop
- ■ train station
- ● bus service
- 🏧 ATM

Cum. stage distance (km)	hotel	campsite	refreshments	grocery	outdoor	train	bus	ATM
0km	⊙		🍴				●	
	⊙		🍴	⊕	✪	■	●	🏧
4km	⊙		🍴	⊕			●	🏧
11.3km								
			🍴				●	
			🍴				●	
	⊙		🍴					
	⊙		🍴	⊕			●	
10.6km								
0.7km	⊙							
7.8km	⊙	▲	🍴					
		▲	🍴					
	⊙		🍴					
	⊙	▲	🍴					
15.5km		▲	🍴				●	
19.3km	⊙		🍴	⊕			●	🏧
7.1km							●	
	⊙		🍴					
7.6km			🍴					

WALKING THE SARSEN WAY

Stage	Place	Walking time	Cum. stage time	Distance (km)
5	**Netheravon**	**14½hr**	**3¼hr**	**52.1km**
5	Bulford	16½hr	2hr	59.6km
5	*Durrington*			*59.6km (+0.5km)*
6	**Amesbury**	**17½hr**	**3hr**	**62.7km**
6	Great Durnford	18¾hr	1¼hr	66.9km
6	*Lake*			*66.9km (+1.1km)*
6	Upper Woodford	19¼hr	½hr	68.5km
6	*High Post*			*68.5km (+2.3km)*
6	Old Sarum	20¾hr	1½hr	73.7km
6	*Longhedge / Old Sarum*			*73.7km (+1.4km)*
6	**Salisbury**	**22hr**	**4½hr**	**79km**
Avebury loop				
2	**Cross-junction with the Herepath/Green Street (Wessex Ridgeway)**	**0hr**	**0hr**	**0km**
2	Avebury	¾hr	¾hr	2.5km
2	*Avebury Trusloe*			*2.5km (+0.8km)*
2	*Beckhampton*			*2.5km (+1.8km)*
3	**Overton Hill**	**1¼hr**	**1¼hr**	**4.8km**
Cranborne Droves Way				
1	**Salisbury**	**0hr**	**0hr**	**0km**
1	*Coombe Bissett*			*8km (+1.7km)*

Appendix D – Stage Facilities Planner

Cum. stage distance (km)	Facilities							
10.9km	🛖		🍴	🚉			🔵	🛏
7.5km	🛖		🍴	🚉			🔵	
	🛖		🍴	🚉			🔵	🛏
10.6km	🛖		🍴	🚉			🔵	🛏
4.3km	🛖		🍴				🔵	
	🛖							
5.9km			🍴					
	🛖						🔵	
11.1km			🍴				🔵	
				🚉				🛏
16.3km	🛖	🟢	🍴	🚉	😀	🔴	🔵	🛏
0km								
2.5km	🛖		🍴				🔵	🛏
	🛖							
	🛖		🍴				🔵	
4.8km								
0km	🛖	🟢	🍴	🚉	😀	🔴	🔵	🛏
			🍴	🚉			🔵	🛏

WALKING THE SARSEN WAY

Stage	Place	Walking time	Cum. stage time	Distance (km)
1	*Bishopstone*			10.1km (+1.7km)
1	*Broad Chalke*			14.2km (+3.2km)
2	**Cow Down Hill**	**5hr**	**5hr**	**17.3km**
2	*Bowerchalke*			17.3km (+2km)
2	*Woodminton*			18.9km (+1.2km)
2	*Ebbesbourne Wake*			20.6km (+2.7km)
2	*Alvediston*			22.1km (+1.9km)
2	*Berwick St John*			26.1km (+1.9km)
2	*Tollard Royal*			26.3km (+1.9km)
2	**Win Green**			*28km*
2	Ludwell	8¾hr	3¾hr	30.9km
2	**Shaftesbury**	**10½hr**	**5½hr**	**36.5km**

Notes

Off-route distance is via shortest route; note that some places (eg, Avebury) are visited on the optional loops.

Bus services may be limited and/or irregular, and may not operate on Sundays.

There are no water taps along the route.

The ATMs in Upavon, Netheravon, Coombe Bisset and Ludwell are in Post Offices, so are only accessible when the Post Offices are open.

Appendix D – Stage facilities planner

Cum. stage distance (km)	Facilities						
			🍴			⬛	
	⛺		🍴	🍽		⬛	
17.35km							
	⛺					⬛	
		🔺					
			🍴			⬛	
						⬛	
			🍴			⬛	
	⛺		🍴				
13.65km	⛺		🍴	🍽		⬛	🚆
19.2km	⛺	🔺	🍴	🍽	🟥	⬛	🚆

NOTES

NOTES

DOWNLOAD THE GPX FILES

All the routes in this guide are available for download from:

www.cicerone.co.uk/1126/GPX

as standard format GPX files. You should be able to load them into most online GPX systems and mobile devices, whether GPS or smartphone. You may need to convert the file into your preferred format using a conversion programme such as gpsvisualizer.com or one of the many other such websites and programmes.

When you follow this link, you will be asked for your email address and where you purchased the guidebook, and have the option to subscribe to the Cicerone e-newsletter.

www.cicerone.co.uk

LISTING OF CICERONE GUIDES

BRITISH ISLES CHALLENGES, COLLECTIONS AND ACTIVITIES
Cycling Land's End to John o' Groats
Great Walks on the England Coast Path
The Big Rounds
The Book of the Bivvy
The Book of the Bothy
The Mountains of England and Wales: Vol 1 Wales
The Mountains of England and Wales: Vol 2 England
The National Trails
Walking the End to End Trail

SHORT WALKS SERIES
Short Walks Hadrian's Wall
Short Walks in Arnside and Silverdale
Short Walks in Cornwall: Falmouth and the Lizard
Short Walks in Dumfries and Galloway
Short Walks in Nidderdale
Short Walks in Pembrokeshire: Tenby and the south
Short Walks in the South Downs: Brighton, Eastbourne and Arundel
Short Walks in the Surrey Hills
Short Walks Lake District – Coniston and Langdale
Short Walks Lake District: Keswick, Borrowdale and Buttermere
Short Walks Lake District: Windermere Ambleside and Grasmere
Short Walks on the Malvern Hills
Short Walks Winchester

SCOTLAND
Ben Nevis and Glen Coe
Cycling in the Hebrides
Cycling the North Coast 500
Great Mountain Days in Scotland
Mountain Biking in Southern and Central Scotland
Mountain Biking in West and North West Scotland
Not the West Highland Way Scotland
Scotland's Best Small Mountains
Scotland's Mountain Ridges
Scottish Wild Country Backpacking
Skye's Cuillin Ridge Traverse
The Borders Abbeys Way
The Great Glen Way
The Great Glen Way Map Booklet
The Hebridean Way
The Hebrides
The Isle of Mull
The Isle of Skye
The Skye Trail
The Southern Upland Way
The West Highland Way
The West Highland Way Map Booklet
Walking Ben Lawers, Rannoch and Atholl
Walking in the Cairngorms
Walking in the Pentland Hills
Walking in the Scottish Borders
Walking in the Southern Uplands
Walking in Torridon, Fisherfield, Fannichs and An Teallach
Walking Loch Lomond and the Trossachs
Walking on Arran
Walking on Harris and Lewis
Walking on Jura, Islay and Colonsay
Walking on Rum and the Small Isles
Walking on the Orkney and Shetland Isles
Walking on Uist and Barra
Walking the Cape Wrath Trail
Walking the Corbetts
  Vol 1 South of the Great Glen
  Vol 2 North of the Great Glen
Walking the Galloway Hills
Walking the John o' Groats Trail
Walking the Munros
  Vol 1 – Southern, Central and Western Highlands
  Vol 2 – Northern Highlands and the Cairngorms
Winter Climbs in the Cairngorms
Winter Climbs: Ben Nevis and Glen Coe

NORTHERN ENGLAND ROUTES
Cycling the Reivers Route
Cycling the Way of the Roses
Hadrian's Cycleway
Hadrian's Wall Path
Hadrian's Wall Path Map Booklet
The Coast to Coast Cycle Route
The Coast to Coast Walk
The Coast to Coast Walk Map Booklet
The Pennine Way
The Pennine Way Map Booklet
Walking the Dales Way
Walking the Dales Way Map Booklet

NORTH-EAST ENGLAND, YORKSHIRE DALES AND PENNINES
Cycling in the Yorkshire Dales
Great Mountain Days in the Pennines
Mountain Biking in the Yorkshire Dales
The Cleveland Way and the Yorkshire Wolds Way
The North York Moors
Trail and Fell Running in the Yorkshire Dales
Walking in County Durham
Walking in Northumberland
Walking in the North Pennines
Walking in the Yorkshire Dales:
  North and East
  South and West
Walking St Cuthbert's Way
Walking St Oswald's Way and Northumberland Coast Path

NORTH-WEST ENGLAND AND THE ISLE OF MAN
Cycling the Pennine Bridleway
Isle of Man Coastal Path
The Lancashire Cycleway
The Lune Valley and Howgills
Walking in Cumbria's Eden Valley
Walking in Lancashire
Walking in the Forest of Bowland and Pendle
Walking on the Isle of Man
Walking on the West Pennine Moors
Walking the Ribble Way
Walks in Silverdale and Arnside

LAKE DISTRICT
Bikepacking in the Lake District
Cycling in the Lake District
Great Mountain Days in the Lake District
Joss Naylor's Lakes, Meres and Waters of the Lake District
Lake District Winter Climbs
Lake District:
  High Level and Fell Walks
  Low Level and Lake Walks
Mountain Biking in the Lake District
Outdoor Adventures with Children – Lake District
Scrambles in the Lake District –
  North
  South
Trail and Fell Running in the Lake District
Walking The Cumbria Way
Walking the Lake District Fells –
  Borrowdale
  Buttermere
  Coniston
  Keswick
  Langdale
  Mardale and the Far East
  Patterdale
  Wasdale
Walking the Tour of the Lake District

DERBYSHIRE, PEAK DISTRICT AND MIDLANDS
Cycling in the Peak District
Dark Peak Walks

Walking in Derbyshire
Walking in the Peak District –
　White Peak East
　White Peak West

SOUTHERN ENGLAND

20 Classic Sportive Rides in
　South East England
　South West England
Cycling in the Cotswolds
Mountain Biking on the
　North Downs
　South Downs
Suffolk Coast and Heath Walks
The Cotswold Way
The Cotswold Way Map Booklet
The Kennet and Avon Canal
The Lea Valley Walk
The North Downs Way
The North Downs Way Map Booklet
The Peddars Way and Norfolk
　Coast Path
The Pilgrims' Way
The Ridgeway National Trail
The Ridgeway National Trail
　Map Booklet
The South Downs Way
The South Downs Way Map Booklet
The Thames Path
The Thames Path Map Booklet
The Two Moors Way
The Two Moors Way Map Booklet
Walking Hampshire's Test Way
Walking in Cornwall
Walking in Essex
Walking in Kent
Walking in London
Walking in Norfolk
Walking in the Chilterns
Walking in the Cotswolds
Walking in the Isles of Scilly
Walking in the New Forest
Walking in the North Wessex Downs
Walking on Dartmoor
Walking on Guernsey
Walking on Jersey
Walking on the Isle of Wight
Walking the Dartmoor Way
Walking the Jurassic Coast
Walking the South West Coast Path
Walking the South West Coast Path
　Map Booklets
　– Vol 1: Minehead to St Ives
　– Vol 2: St Ives to Plymouth
　– Vol 3: Plymouth to Poole
Walks in the South Downs
　National Park

WALES AND WELSH BORDERS

Cycle Touring in Wales
Cycling Lon Las Cymru
Great Mountain Days in Snowdonia
Hillwalking in Shropshire
Mountain Walking in Snowdonia
Offa's Dyke Path
Offa's Dyke Path Map Booklet
Ridges of Snowdonia
Scrambles in Snowdonia
Snowdonia: 30 Low-level and
　Easy Walks
　– North
　– South
The Cambrian Way
The Pembrokeshire Coast Path
The Pembrokeshire Coast Path
　Map Booklet
The Snowdonia Way
Walking Glyndwr's Way
Walking in Carmarthenshire
Walking in Pembrokeshire
Walking in the Brecon Beacons
Walking in the Forest of Dean
Walking in the Wye Valley
Walking on Gower
Walking the Severn Way
Walking the Shropshire Way
Walking the Wales Coast Path

INTERNATIONAL CHALLENGES, COLLECTIONS AND ACTIVITIES

Europe's High Points
Walking the Via Francigena
　Pilgrim Route – Part 1

AFRICA

Kilimanjaro
Walking in the Drakensberg
Walks and Scrambles in the
　Moroccan Anti-Atlas

ALPS CROSS-BORDER ROUTES

100 Hut Walks in the Alps
Alpine Ski Mountaineering
　Vol 1 – Western Alps
The Karnischer Hohenweg
The Tour of the Bernina
Trail Running – Chamonix and the
　Mont Blanc region
Trekking Chamonix to Zermatt
Trekking in the Alps
Trekking in the Silvretta and
　Ratikon Alps
Trekking Munich to Venice
Trekking the Tour du Mont Blanc
Trekking the Tour du Mont Blanc
　Map Booklet
Walking in the Alps

PYRENEES AND FRANCE/SPAIN CROSS-BORDER ROUTES

Shorter Treks in the Pyrenees
The Pyrenean Haute Route
The Pyrenees
Trekking the GR11 Trail
Walks and Climbs in the Pyrenees

AUSTRIA

Innsbruck Mountain Adventures
Trekking Austria's Adlerweg
Trekking in Austria's Hohe Tauern
Trekking in Austria's Zillertal Alps
Trekking in the Stubai Alps
Walking in Austria
Walking in the Salzkammergut:
　the Austrian Lake District

EASTERN EUROPE

The Danube Cycleway Vol 2
The High Tatras
The Mountains of Romania
Walking in Hungary

FRANCE, BELGIUM AND LUXEMBOURG

Camino de Santiago – Via Podiensis
Chamonix Mountain Adventures
Cycle Touring in France
Cycling London to Paris
Cycling the Canal de la Garonne
Cycling the Canal du Midi
Cycling the Route des Grandes Alpes
Mont Blanc Walks
Mountain Adventures in
　the Maurienne
Short Treks on Corsica
The Elbe Cycle Route
The GR5 Trail
The GR5 Trail – Benelux and
　Lorraine
The GR5 Trail – Vosges and Jura
The Grand Traverse of the
　Massif Central
The Moselle Cycle Route
The River Loire Cycle Route
The River Rhone Cycle Route
Trekking in the Vanoise
Trekking the Cathar Way
Trekking the GR10
Trekking the GR20 Corsica
Trekking the Robert Louis
　Stevenson Trail
Via Ferratas of the French Alps
Walking in Provence – East
Walking in Provence – West
Walking in the Ardennes
Walking in the Auvergne
Walking in the Briançonnais
Walking in the Dordogne
Walking in the Haute Savoie: North
Walking in the Haute Savoie: South
Walking on Corsica
Walking the Brittany Coast Path

GERMANY

Hiking and Cycling in the
　Black Forest
The Danube Cycleway Vol 1
The Rhine Cycle Route
The Westweg
Walking in the Bavarian Alps

IRELAND

The Wild Atlantic Way and Western Ireland
Walking the Wicklow Way

ITALY

Alta Via – Trekking in the Dolomites – Vols 1&2
Day Walks in the Dolomites
Italy's Grande Traversata delle Alpi
Italy's Sibillini National Park
Ski Touring and Snowshoeing in the Dolomites
The Way of St Francis
Trekking in the Apennines
Trekking the Giants' Trail: Alta Via 1 through the Italian Pennine Alps
Via Ferratas of the Italian Dolomites – Vols 1&2
Walking in Abruzzo
Walking in Italy's Cinque Terre
Walking in Italy's Stelvio National Park
Walking in Sicily
Walking in the Aosta Valley
Walking in the Dolomites
Walking in Tuscany
Walking in Umbria
Walking Lake Como and Maggiore
Walking Lake Garda and Iseo
Walking on the Amalfi Coast
Walking the Via Francigena Pilgrim Route – Parts 2&3
Walks and Treks in the Maritime Alps

MEDITERRANEAN

The High Mountains of Crete
Trekking in Greece
Walking and Trekking in Zagori
Walking and Trekking on Corfu
Walking in Cyprus
Walking on Malta
Walking on the Greek Islands – the Cyclades

NEW ZEALAND AND AUSTRALIA

Hiking the Overland Track

NORTH AMERICA

Hiking and Cycling the California Missions Trail
The John Muir Trail
The Pacific Crest Trail

SOUTH AMERICA

Aconcagua and the Southern Andes
Hiking and Biking Peru's Inca Trails
Trekking in Torres del Paine

SCANDINAVIA, ICELAND AND GREENLAND

Hiking in Norway – South
Trekking in Greenland – The Arctic Circle Trail
Trekking the Kungsleden
Walking and Trekking in Iceland

SLOVENIA, CROATIA, SERBIA, MONTENEGRO AND ALBANIA

Hiking Slovenia's Juliana Trail
Mountain Biking in Slovenia
The Islands of Croatia
The Julian Alps of Slovenia
The Mountains of Montenegro
The Peaks of the Balkans Trail
The Slovene Mountain Trail
Walking in Slovenia: The Karavanke
Walks and Treks in Croatia

SPAIN AND PORTUGAL

Camino de Santiago: Camino Frances
Coastal Walks in Andalucia
Costa Blanca Mountain Adventures
Cycling the Camino de Santiago
Cycling the Ruta Via de la Plata
Mountain Walking in Mallorca
Mountain Walking in Southern Catalunya
Portugal's Rota Vicentina
Spain's Sendero Historico: The GR1
The Andalucian Coast to Coast Walk
The Camino del Norte and Camino Primitivo
The Camino Ingles and Ruta do Mar
The Camino Portugues
The Mountains Around Nerja
The Mountains of Ronda and Grazalema
The Sierras of Extremadura
Trekking in Mallorca
Trekking in the Canary Islands
Trekking the GR7 in Andalucia
Walking and Trekking in the Sierra Nevada
Walking in Andalucia
Walking in Catalunya – Barcelona
Walking in Catalunya – Girona Pyrenees
Walking in Portugal
Walking in the Algarve
Walking in the Picos de Europa
Walking La Via de la Plata and Camino Sanabres
Walking on Gran Canaria
Walking on La Gomera and El Hierro
Walking on La Palma
Walking on Lanzarote and Fuerteventura
Walking on Madeira
Walking on Tenerife
Walking on the Azores
Walking on the Costa Blanca
Walking the Camino dos Faros

SWITZERLAND

Switzerland's Jura Crest Trail
The Swiss Alps
Tour of the Jungfrau Region
Trekking the Swiss Via Alpina
Walking in the Bernese Oberland – Jungfrau region
Walking in the Engadine – Switzerland
Walking in the Valais
Walking in Ticino
Walking in Zermatt and Saas-Fee

CHINA, JAPAN AND ASIA

Hiking and Trekking in the Japan Alps and Mount Fuji
Hiking in Hong Kong
Japan's Kumano Kodo Pilgrimage
Trekking in Tajikistan

HIMALAYA

Annapurna
8000 metres
Everest: A Trekker's Guide
Trekking in Bhutan
Trekking in Ladakh
Trekking in the Himalaya
Trekking in the Karakoram

MOUNTAIN LITERATURE

A Walk in the Clouds
Abode of the Gods
Fifty Years of Adventure
The Pennine Way – the Path, the People, the Journey
Unjustifiable Risk?
Unjustifiable Risk?

TECHNIQUES

Fastpacking
Geocaching in the UK
Map and Compass
Outdoor Photography
The Mountain Hut Book

MINI GUIDES

Alpine Flowers
Navigation
Pocket First Aid and Wilderness Medicine
Snow

For full information on all our guides, books and eBooks,
visit our website:
www.cicerone.co.uk

CICERONE

Trust Cicerone to guide your next adventure, wherever it may be around the world...

Discover guides for hiking, mountain walking, backpacking, trekking, trail running, cycling and mountain biking, ski touring, climbing and scrambling in Britain, Europe and worldwide.

Connect with Cicerone online and find inspiration.

- buy books and ebooks
- articles, advice and trip reports
- podcasts and live events
- GPX files and updates
- regular newsletter

cicerone.co.uk